Listen Children

There was a little path beside the rocky road, and Mrs. Flowers walked in front swinging her arms and picking her way over the stones.

"Come and walk along with me, Marguerite." I couldn't have refused even if I wanted to. She pronounced my name so nicely. Or more correctly, she spoke each word with such clarity that I was certain a foreigner who didn't understand English would have understood her.

"Now no one is going to make you talk—possibly no one can. But bear in mind, language is man's way of communicating with his fellow man and it is language alone which separates him from the lower animals." That was a totally new idea to me, and I would need time to think about it.

from *I Know Why the Caged Bird Sings*
by Maya Angelou

Bantam Books of Related Interest
Ask your bookseller for the books you have missed

Listen Children

An Anthology of Black Literature

Edited by Dorothy S. Strickland
With a Foreword by Coretta Scott King
Illustrated by Leo and Diane Dillon

A Bantam Skylark Book®
Toronto · New York · London · Sydney

RL 5, 010-014

LISTEN CHILDREN
A Bantam Skylark Book / April 1982

*Skylark Books is a registered trademark of Bantam Books, Inc.,
Registered in U.S. Patent and Trademark Office and elsewhere.*

COPYRIGHT NOTICES AND ACKNOWLEDGMENTS

Bantam Books are published by Bantam Books, Inc. Its trademark, consisting of the words "Bantam Books" and the portrayal of a rooster, is Registered in U.S. Patent and Trademark Office and in other countries. Marca Registrada. Bantam Books, Inc., 666 Fifth Avenue, New York, New York 10103.

PRINTED IN THE UNITED STATES OF AMERICA

0 9 8 7 6 5 4 3 2 1

To my children

Mark
Randy
Michael

D.S.S.

My thanks to M. Jerry Weiss and Judy Gitenstein whose inspiration and advice made this book a reality.

A special thank you to Coretta Scott King, President, The Martin Luther King, Jr. Center for Social Change, for her participation in this book.

Contents

FOREWORD

Literature is a unique resource that articulates and preserves a people's culture. Often it was through literature that my generation grew in our understanding of the past, so that we could gain insight into present events and develop perspectives for the future. Children need and benefit from literary experiences that develop their awareness of themselves as individuals and as part of a cultural family. The literary heritage of a people also benefits those outside that family by developing their appreciation of important differences and similarities of experience. For although literature can never replace actual human interaction, it can deepen the understanding that comes from sharing in the common struggle for human dignity and freedom.

Listen Children brings together the work of many of our most gifted black writers. Their words form a world of energy, pathos, humor, and strength. They are part of an enduring lifeline that affirms our history and perpetuates our identity. This collection of twenty-two pieces is expressly designed to bring that kind of rich literary experience to its readers. It is a much needed offering for children as they search for ways to explain their own existence and question the conditions of society.

I recommend *Listen Children* to everyone—black and white, child and adult—who wishes to share in the documentation of black humanity's efforts toward a better world.

CORETTA SCOTT KING,
President,
The Martin Luther King, Jr.
Center for Social Change

INTRODUCTION

This book is for *all* children. Yes, it is a collection of stories and experiences by black writers addressed to black children who are learning about their heritage. But it is also a collection of writing for all children learning to value themselves. In the process of growing up, understanding yourself comes with reaching out to broaden your understanding of others.

This anthology can be used in the classroom or simply read for enjoyment. The selections here were chosen because they seemed to speak about the ways we grow, about the places we all pass through, and about the new feelings we encounter at each stage. The book touches on four themes, each part of a progressing awareness: Feeling the Joy of Being Me; Feelings about My Roots; Feeling the Pain and Pride of Struggle; and Feelings about Who I Am and What I Want to Be.

The poems and stories in Feeling the Joy of Being Me center on self-awareness and self-acceptance—knowing who you are and feeling good about it. Beginning with the poems of Eloise Greenfield and Gwendolyn Brooks, and a story by Virginia Hamilton, we meet three very different young people, all coming into their own. Sonia Sanchez's delightful poem for a little brother provides the perfect lead-in to "All Around the Mulberry Tree," Kristin Hunter's story of a rural boy's adjustment to life in the big city.

Feeling secure in your world often stems from knowing that you belong to two very special groups—your family and your community. Their traditions, songs, stories, and celebrations all become yours. Feelings about My Roots: Folktales and Folkways explores the rich and vital heritage belonging to blacks throughout the world. Two poems about the ways we are connected to our ancestors and with each other are followed by traditional African folktales.

The history of this country is filled with conflict and great courage. The voices in Feeling the Pain and Pride of Struggle express black strife from slavery to the present search for equality and brotherhood. A play that may be performed or read aloud, *When the Rattlesnake Sounds* takes us into the life of Harriet Tubman as she worked to earn money for the Underground Railroad. A vignette from *Rosa Parks* introduces us to another woman who, more than a hundred years later, continued the spirit and tenacity of that struggle.

Feelings about Who I Am and What I Want to Be focuses on forging your own identity, knowing that you are a unique individual and at the same time, part of a bigger, identifiable group. Here are recollections from the lives of Maya Angelou, Wilma Rudolph, and Stevie Wonder. We meet them as children and teenagers, and we begin to understand where they came from. "December," a poem by Lucille Clifton, is an ending—for a year, for a book, for a cycle of growth that always takes us round to a new beginning.

The voices in this anthology are meant to tell a human story as expressed through the celebration of growing up black. It is certainly about being black and being young, but if there is a moving spirit in this collection, it is one of love.

Listen children . . .

—*Dorothy S. Strickland*

LISTEN
CHILDREN

FEELING THE JOY
OF BEING ME

WAY DOWN IN THE MUSIC

I get way down in the music
Down inside the music
I let it wake me
        take me
Spin me around and make me
Uh-get down

Inside the sound of the Jackson Five
Into the tune of Earth, Wind and Fire
Down in the bass where the beat comes from
Down in the horn and down in the drum
I get down
I get down

I get way down in the music
Down inside the music
I let it wake me
        take me
Spin me around and shake me
I get down, down
I get down

Eloise Greenfield

ANDRE

I had a dream last night. I dreamed
I had to pick a Mother out.
I had to choose a Father too.
At first, I wondered what to do,
There were so many there, it seemed,
Short and tall and thin and stout.

But just before I sprang awake,
I knew what parents I would take.

And this surprised and made me glad:
They were the ones I already had!

Gwendolyn Brooks

HOW JAHDU
BECAME HIMSELF

Virginia Hamilton

Summer had come to the good place called Harlem. The window was open wide in Mama Luka's hot little room. Mama Luka had moved her chair closer to the window. Yes, she had. She had raised her blind so that she could see what happened in the street below.

"Yes, child," she said to Lee Edward, who sat on the floor. "I have seen fifty summers come to that street down there and with each summer will come Jahdu just running along."

"Will I get to see him this summer?" asked Lee Edward.

"You might have a hard time seeing him, Little Brother," Mama Luka said. "Jahdu is never the same."

"Not even his face?" asked Lee Edward. He hoped this time to catch Mama Luka before she had time to think.

"Anyone who has seen the face of Jahdu will tell you *only* that it is never the same," said Mama Luka carefully. "But there is a steady light from his eyes," she said. "There is pride in his face that is always the same."

"I will look for Jahdu," said Lee Edward. "I will look for the pride in every face I see."

5

"You know, I start baking bread in the summertime," Mama Luka told Lee Edward. "I always think that maybe this time Jahdu will stop and visit with me and tell me what he has been up to."

"Has Jahdu ever stopped by to visit with you?" asked Lee Edward.

Mama Luka stared out her window. She spoke softly to Lee Edward. "I am baking bread right now," she said. "I am baking bread and I am hoping."

"I can smell the bread," Lee Edward said. "It smells very good, too."

"Yes, child," said Mama Luka, turning from the window. "I never told you before, but Jahdu was born in an oven beside two loaves of baking bread." Mama Luka smiled. "One loaf baked brown and the other baked black. Jahdu didn't bake at all. But since that time black and brown have been Jahdu's favorite colors and the smell of baking bread is the sweetest smell to him."

Then Lee Edward pointed to the windowsill all of a sudden. Mama Luka understood and she cupped her hands around the place Lee Edward had pointed to. Mama Luka opened her mouth and swallowed what had been in her hands.

"Oh, yes," she said. "Little Brother, that's the best old story you picked out of the air. It makes me feel cool and fresh inside."

"Then tell it," Lee Edward said to Mama Luka.

"I'm getting myself ready," said Mama Luka.

THIS IS THE JAHDU STORY SO COOL AND FRESH THAT MAMA LUKA TOLD TO LEE EDWARD.

Jahdu was running along. He was telling everybody to get out of his way. Everybody always did get out of Jahdu's way. Except this time somebody wouldn't and that somebody was Grass.

Grass lay on the ground in one dull shade of gray as far as the eye could see. Jahdu shouted at him. "Get out of the way, Grass, for Jahdu is coming through."

Grass didn't move at all. No, he didn't. Jahdu lay down on Grass and stretched himself out as far as he could.

"How do you like that, Uncle No-Color?" Jahdu said to Grass. "Jahdu is heavy, isn't he?"

Grass didn't say a word. But Grass couldn't feel the sunlight with Jahdu stretched out on him and he grew cold. And when Jahdu called him Uncle No-Color, he became very angry.

Grass lifted all his young gray blades straight as arrows. He pushed them against Jahdu with all his might. And the strain on his young gray blades turned each and every one of them green. To this day you can tell Grass whenever you chance to see him. For each and every one of his blades is still green.

Well, Jahdu laughed. He got up slowly. He yawned two or three times and gave no more thought to Grass, who had turned green.

Jahdu kept right on running along. He was running eastward, for he had been born in the East. And Jahdu had an idea he might like to be born again into something else. He ran and he ran until he came to dry, hot sand.

"Woogily!" Jahdu whispered. "This sand is hotter than anything I know that is hot."

Jahdu saw Ocean lying as calm as could be on the horizon where the hot sand ended.

Jahdu screamed in his meanest voice. "Hey, Uncle Calm Ocean! Why don't you once in a while get up and give the sand something to cool itself with? Lying around all day, watering the clouds and cooling off the birds. Why don't you get yourself together long enough to help out the hot sand?"

Old Ocean wasn't bad. But he was used to being the biggest somebody around under the sky. He was used to not moving, just lying there as cool and blue as he pleased. Ocean knew he was bigger and wetter and deeper than anything under the sun. And when Jahdu said what he had, all grew still. The wind stopped its blowing. Ocean himself stopped being lazy long enough to think about what Jahdu had said.

All at once Ocean gathered himself together right across his middle. He gave a heave that lifted his body higher than he had ever lifted it before. Ocean started moving from the horizon over the sand in a white, foaming line treetop tall.

"Woogily!" said Jahdu. And he went on running.

Old Ocean leaped right in front of Jahdu. But Ocean didn't catch Jahdu. For Jahdu surely knew how to keep running along. Every time Ocean slid back to the horizon to gather himself together again, Jahdu would run away somewhere else. Ocean would hit the hot sand with all his might only to find that Jahdu had run by.

To this day Ocean keeps on moving up and back and up and back again. He keeps on trying to catch anything passing by.

Jahdu kept right on running along. He was growing tired. He felt like stopping to rest. But he had no friend he could stop along with. He had played so many tricks nobody trusted him.

Mrs. Alligator used to give Jahdu free rides on her back. But not anymore, for Jahdu had come along one time with a can of blue paint on his head. He had put Mrs. Alligator to sleep and then he had painted her skin with two coats of blue paint. The paint hadn't worn off for a year. Now Mrs. Alligator thought Jahdu had manners worse than a crocodile's. Whenever she heard Jahdu running along, she would dive deep to the bottom of her pool. Yes, she would.

Jahdu came alongside a shade tree. The shade tree had leaves as big as elephant's ears. It had a trunk smooth to lean against. So Jahdu sat himself down. He leaned against the tree trunk and rested. He let the leaves as big as elephant's ears fan him. Jahdu soon felt like taking a nap. He was almost asleep when he heard a voice next to him.

"Stranger, kindly move off my tail!" said the voice. "Hey, you, sir, who will lean against a body without a pardon me!"

"Woogily!" said Jahdu, and he jumped five feet away from the tree.

It wasn't the shade tree who had spoken. Shade trees do not speak and do not care who leans against them. It was old Chameleon who had spoken. Chameleon was a lizard six inches long. He had not seen Jahdu for many a month. But when Jahdu said "Woogily!" Chameleon knew him right away.

"Jahdu," Chameleon said, "I wish you would learn to ask somebody when you want to lean on somebody."

Jahdu looked all around. It took him a minute to see the lizard on the tree trunk. Jahdu had always liked Chameleon. Chameleon could change the color of his skin any time he felt like it. If Chameleon sat down on a green leaf, he would turn himself green and nobody could tell he was sitting on the leaf. If he wanted to sit on a flat stone, he would turn himself the color of the flat stone. And nobody need know he was resting awhile.

At last Jahdu saw Chameleon on the trunk of the shade tree. Chameleon was brown as was the dark brown tree trunk.

"Well, how are you doing?" Jahdu said, coming closer.

"You stay right where you are!" shouted Chameleon. "Don't come any nearer until you promise you won't tie my tail in a knot."

"Oh, my goodness," Jahdu said, sitting down.

"I mean what I say," Chameleon told Jahdu. "The last time you tied my tail up I had an awful time getting it untied."

"How *did* you get it untied?" Jahdu wanted to know. He spoke to the lizard in his kindest voice. For Jahdu knew now that he wanted something special from the lizard.

"Never you mind how I got myself loose," said Chameleon. "You just promise."

So Jahdu promised. Then he and the lizard sat against the trunk of the shade tree.

"I've just been running along," Jahdu told his friend Chameleon.

"All right," said Chameleon.

"I had a little fun with Grass," said Jahdu.

"That's good," said the lizard. "Grass is always so gray and sad."

"Not anymore," Jahdu said. "Grass is now green as he can be!"

"All right," Chameleon said. "Green is brighter than gray."

"I had a little fun with Ocean," Jahdu told his friend.

"That's all right," said Chameleon. "Ocean always did lie too far back on the horizon."

"Not anymore," Jahdu told him. "Now Ocean rises treetop tall. He runs over the hot sand hilltop high and then he falls down trying to catch anything running along."

"That's good, too," said the lizard. "Now the hot sand will get a chance to cool itself."

"So I have stopped awhile from running along," said Jahdu.

"All right," Chameleon said.

"I have stopped and now I know why I was running along and what I want from you," said Jahdu.

"Tell me then," said the lizard.

"I want to know how you work your magic," said Jahdu.

"You already have your own magic," Chameleon told Jahdu. "You can put anything to sleep and wake anything up again."

"But I need to know the magic you have," said Jahdu to his friend.

"What magic is that?" Chameleon asked Jahdu.

"You can change to look like a stone or even a leaf," Jahdu told him.

"Sure, I can," said the lizard, "but I can't let you do that, too."

"Well, I know you can't, my friend," Jahdu said. "I only want to know how you do it. If I know how it is you can change and hide, maybe I can learn how to just change into something else."

"Change into what?" Chameleon wanted to know.

"Change myself into whatever I want," Jahdu told him. "If I see a deer, I can be a deer running through the woods. If I see a fox, I can be as swift and clever as a fox."

Chameleon smiled. "It's not hard," he told Jahdu. "I will tell you what I do. With a bit of practice maybe it will work for you."

"Tell me then," said Jahdu.

"First I see a place where I want to sit," Chameleon said. "Then I think about what it feels like sitting there. Next I run as fast as I can to get there. And then I sit. And the color of the thing I'm sitting on comes over me right away."

"That's all you do?" Jahdu asked. "Woogily!" he said. "Changing is going to be easy!"

Suddenly Jahdu looked unhappy. "How am I going to run fast enough to catch up with a deer and climb on his back?" he asked the lizard.

"Maybe you won't have to run at all," said Chameleon. "Maybe you will only need to see the deer running fast."

"Then what?" Jahdu asked.

"Then you think hard," said Chameleon. "You say to

yourself, 'Jahdu is running as fast as that deer. Jahdu is on that deer. Jahdu *is* that deer!' "

"Woogily!" said Jahdu.

"Try it," Chameleon told Jahdu.

Jahdu left his friend Chameleon dozing against the trunk of the shade tree. Jahdu went running along. He had not seen anything yet that he wanted to be. He was still running eastward to where he had been born.

"The first thing I see that I like, I will be," Jahdu said to himself. And he kept right on running along.

Jahdu came to an island. The island had buildings higher than high. Jahdu liked the buildings. Yes, he did.

He said, "Woogily!" and kept on running. "I'm going to make myself into a building."

Jahdu picked out for himself a building higher than a hilltop. He thought very hard. "Jahdu is running to that building," he said to himself. "Jahdu is on top of that building. Jahdu *is* that building!"

Jahdu became a building made of steel and concrete. He was very tall, but he could not move. Jahdu did not like standing still.

"Woogily!" said Jahdu. He thought very quickly and he said to himself, "Jahdu is jumping off this building. Jahdu is running away from this building. Jahdu is not a building anymore!"

Jahdu kept right on running along. He ran and he ran through the city on an island. He saw a stray cat and he became the cat. But Jahdu didn't like being a cat. He was always hungry. He was sick and he was tired and he slept where he could. Jahdu was thrown out of a supermarket for trying to get at the frozen fish.

"Woogily!" said Jahdu. "Cats have a hard time getting along. Jahdu is jumping off this cat. Jahdu is running faster than this cat. Jahdu is not a cat anymore!"

Jahdu kept on running. He saw an orange-and-black taxicab.

"Woogily!" said Jahdu. "I'm going to be that taxicab." And so he was.

Now Jahdu was busy taking people from one place to another. But he didn't much like being a taxicab. People sat down too hard on his seats and tracked dirt in on his floor. People were afraid when he went very fast. Jahdu worked for long hours. Yes, he did. And the bright lights of the city hurt his eyes.

"Jahdu is jumping off this taxicab," Jahdu said at the end of a long day. "Jahdu is moving faster than that pretty orange-and-black taxicab. Jahdu is not a taxicab anymore!"

The taxicab drove away. Jahdu kept right on running along. He found himself in a fine, good place called Harlem. Yes, he did.

"Woogily!" said Jahdu. "All the people here are brown and black."

Jahdu came upon a group of children playing in a playground. He saw a small, black boy who was running around making noise.

"Woogily!" said Jahdu. "Jahdu is running as fast as that black child. Jahdu is jumping on that black child. Jahdu *is* that black child!"

Black was Jahdu's favorite color and Jahdu was now a strong, black child. He didn't own a baseball or a bat. But he had a dog. Yes, Jahdu did. And the dog's name was Rufus. And the dog was black all over, just like Jahdu. Jahdu had a sister and a brother too. And Jahdu had a good time in the city on the island.

Jahdu was happy. He was a strong, black boy. For a while he stayed in the neighborhood, just enjoying himself.

THIS IS THE END OF THE JAHDU STORY SO COOL AND FRESH THAT MAMA LUKA TOLD TO THE CHILD, LEE EDWARD.

"You picked the story," Mama Luka said. "It was a good story and Jahdu was happy being a strong, black boy."

"The way I am happy?" asked Lee Edward.

"Just the way you are happy," said Mama Luka.

"Did the strong, black boy have the Jahdu magic?" asked Lee Edward.

"The strong, black boy was still a small, black boy," said Mama Luka. "And, Little Brother, a small, black boy doesn't have too much magic, even when he's Jahdu. He could put his mama to sleep by making her read him one storybook after another. And he could wake his papa up fast enough by saying he had been a building once upon a time. But he didn't have much more magic than that."

"I don't see how Jahdu of all the Jahdu stories could like being a small, black child," said Lee Edward. "I would think he'd rather be a building."

"You think about it for awhile," Mama Luka told Lee Edward. "I'll take myself a little nap for five or six minutes." Mama Luka always did like sleeping after telling a good Jahdu story.

Mama Luka went right to sleep in her chair and sitting on her long black braid. The smell of baking bread was strong and sweet in the room.

Lee Edward went to Mama Luka's kitchen, not much bigger than a closet, on one side of the room. He peeked into the oven. The large loaf of bread he found had baked brown and was done. Lee Edward took the loaf of bread out of the oven and placed it on the counter. He turned off the oven and stood sniffing the bread that smelled sweeter than anything. And then Lee Edward lay on his back on the floor beside Mama Luka's chair and thought about Jahdu.

Pretty soon Lee Edward closed his eyes and smiled. A little later he opened his eyes and laughed. He knew why Jahdu was happy being a strong, black boy.

Lee Edward imagined Jahdu's changing from a strong, black boy into a bigger, stronger boy. As Jahdu grew, he had more and more magic power. Something Mama Luka had said about Jahdu came to him.

"There is pride in his face that is always the same."

Little Brother had to smile.

"Once he's grown up he'll be a black Jahdu with all his power," whispered Lee Edward.

He pointed to a space of air close to Mama Luka's right foot. He thought he felt himself growing.

"I can have the pride and the power, too," Lee Edward said, and he waited for Mama Luka to wake up.

TO P. J. (2 YRS OLD WHO SED WRITE A POEM FOR ME IN PORTLAND, OREGON)

if i cud ever write a
poem as beautiful as u
little 2/yr/old/brotha,
i wud laugh, jump, leap
up and touch the stars
cuz u be the poem i try for
each time i pick up a pen and paper.
u. and Morani and Mungu
be our blue/blk/stars that
will shine on our lives and
makes us finally BE.
if i cud ever write a poem as beautiful
as u, little 2/yr/old/brotha,
poetry wud go out of bizness.

Sonia Sanchez

17

ALL AROUND THE MULBERRY TREE

Kristin Hunter

When we first came up here from Wrightsville, Georgia, I thought I'd like living in the Franklin Delano Roosevelt Projects. After all, my name is Roosevelt too. Roosevelt Green. With a name like that I could pretend the whole place was mine.

Turns out, not even one corner of our apartment belongs to us. It's impossible to live there the way normal people do in a normal place like Wrightsville.

I thought being twelve stories up in the air would make me feel free, like a bird. And great, like the King of the Mountain. But living high brings me down. Cause every time you put one foot in front of the other, you break a rule.

There's a rule for everything in the projects. Times to put out your trash. Times and places to do your laundry. No running up and down stairs. Everyone under sixteen inside by nine o'clock. Just like jail.

The projects even have a warden, who is called the Superintendent. And each building has a spy who reports to him. The spy gets free rent for snooping and ratting on the other tenants. Mostly you never know who the spy in

18

your building is. But we found out pretty quick that ours was Mrs. Broadnax.

Mrs. Broadnax is a skinny old widow lady with silver-rimmed dark glasses and two gold front teeth and a sly, crooked smile. She always has a hat on. I don't know where she finds them ugly hats. I don't know where she got them glasses, either. They're the darkest I ever seen. But they help her by hiding her eyes. She never looks straight at you when she's talking to you because she's too busy writing up the report in her head.

The trouble with Mrs. Broadnax started because Mom wanted to talk to her friend Mrs. Gaddie. Mrs. Gaddie lives right under us in 11-A. She is from Georgia too. Her home is in Waycross, which is a long way from Wrightsville. But up here, the hundred miles between our home towns seems a lot closer than the one floor between our apartments.

Every day when Mom was ready to talk, she would bang a broom handle on the floor. Back would come a knocking from below. One knock meant, "No, I'm too busy now." Two knocks meant, "Yes, let's have a visit."

If there were two knocks Mom would stick her head out the window and yell down, "How you feelin' today, Essie?"

And Mrs. Gaddie would stick her head out and answer, "No use in complainin', Rosine."

And they would go on like that till they ran out of things to talk about. Or till one of them decided she had something else to do.

One of the things they rapped about a lot was the misery of living in the projects and always finding out you broke some rule. And what they would do to the person who was ratting on them if they ever found out who it was.

I guess that's why Mrs. Broadnax about had a fit when she walked by and heard them. Or else she was just jealous because she didn't have a friend.

Anyway, in five minutes she was knocking on our door.

"Mrs. Green," she said, "you simply cannot hang out of your window like that. If you keep on doing it, you and your family will have to move."

"What are people supposed to do up here?" Mom complained. "This place don't have no front stoops to sit on. And no back porches, either. How's a person going to be sociable?"

"Visit your friend in her apartment," Mrs. Broadnax said.

"I can't go down there and leave these children," Mom said. She wasn't talking about my brother Cephas and me. We're big enough to take care of ourselves. She meant Carmen and Larisse, who are two and four.

"Invite her up here, then."

"She can't come. Her babies are even smaller than mine."

"I don't know what to suggest, then."

"Well, I do. I suggest you take yourself out of my apartment and mind your own business."

Mrs. Broadnax did just that. But she knew she had won.

We knew it, too. It was clear Mrs. Broadnax was a big shot in the projects. It had to be her who had caused all those notes from the Superintendent to appear in our mailbox. Telling us to get rid of our cat because pets weren't allowed. Making Cephas take his school artwork down from our front door. Warning us not to play records with the door open, even on a hot night when we needed air.

Dad had been against Mrs. Broadnax and on our side all those other times. But he wasn't much help in this.

"She's right," he told Mom when he got home. "I don't want you falling out that window and breaking your neck. If you have to see Essie Gaddie, go to her apartment. You can send the children outdoors."

And he went back to eating his watermelon. I guess he felt he had a right to enjoy it in peace, after lugging it up the whole twelve flights of stairs because the elevator was broken again. It was the first watermelon we'd had since we came up North. Getting it home was such hard work, I figured it might be the last.

I saved some seeds and slipped them in my pocket. I planned to put them with my other souvenirs of home: the palmetto leaf, the piece of sugar cane, the hairs from our horse Nellie's tail, the peach pits and pecans from the trees in our yard. I keep these things to help me remember how good life was down home, even though Daddy wasn't making no money there.

The next day, Mom didn't bang on the floor as usual. Nor did she stick her head out the window.

Instead, she told us, "You Roosevelt, you Cephas, take your sisters outside and play with them. Don't let them out of your sight. I'm going down to visit Mrs. Gaddie."

We were happy. That little patch of ground behind our building wasn't even big enough for Nellie to lie down on. But at least it was *ground*, and grass was coming up on it. And right in the center of the grass was a little mulberry tree just turning green.

Living in the city with all its concrete, you forget to notice when winter is over and it is spring. Now we had noticed, and we felt like celebrating. First we took off our shoes. Man! but that grass felt good under our bare feet. Then I took my sisters' hands and led them to the tree. We skipped around it, singing:

> All around the mulberry tree,
> The monkey chases the weasel.

We had just about forgot we were in the city when that mean old Mrs. Broadnax came by. In her blue coat and hat she looked just like a cop.

"Children, what are you doing? Don't you see that 'Keep Off the Grass' sign? Get away from there!"

Carmen and Larisse went on skipping and singing, "The monkey chases the weasel."

"*You* are the monkeys," Mrs. Broadnax said. "You come up here from the country and act just like animals."

"You ain't our mother," I told her.

"No, but I can talk to her," Mrs. Broadnax said. "And I will."

And sure enough, she did, later on that day.

Mom was ready for her. "What you mean, calling my children monkeys and animals?"

"They have no respect for property," Mrs. Broadnax said. "That lawn has just been planted. It is not for anybody to walk on. It is for everybody to look at and enjoy."

"That ain't what it's for where *I* come from," Mom told her. "Where I come from, the earth is for people to use. And running and jumping on it is the healthiest thing children can do."

"Well, you're not down there any more. You're in the city now," Mrs. Broadnax said.

"Yes, and what's wrong with it is too many people like you. Give you people a little job, a little money, and you think you own the earth. Next thing you know we'll have to ask your permission to breathe."

"Don't say you weren't warned," Mrs. Broadnax said.

"I won't," said Mom. But I think she was sick of Mrs. Broadnax and her rules, because the next day she sent us outside again without a word about what we could or couldn't do.

Larisse and Carmen had brought spoons this time. They had a lot of fun digging in the ground while me and Cephas climbed the tree.

Then Larisse called us down. "Let's pretend we planting a garden," she cried, waving her spoon. Larisse is old enough to remember our fields down home.

I pulled the watermelon seeds out of my pocket. There were eight of them. Larisse and Carmen had dug six holes around the tree. I dropped a seed in each hole and still had two left over for my collection.

We covered the seeds with dirt. Then we went back to climbing the tree—all of us except Carmen, cause she's too little. But when all three of us got on the same limb, it snapped.

We wasn't hurt. It was such a little tree, we didn't have far to fall. But when we got up from the grass and brushed ourselves off, there was Mrs. Broadnax watching us—not saying a word, just smiling her sneaky little smile.

That night when Dad got home from work he found a

note from the Superintendent in our mailbox. He would
have to pay an eighty-dollar fine.

He waved the note at Mom. "It says here I have been
warned not to let the kids tear up the lawn. What does it
mean?"

"What it says," she said calmly. "That Broadnax
battle-ax came up here yesterday and said to keep the kids
off the grass."

"And you let them play there again anyway?"

"I did," said Mom. "Nobody is going to tell me how
to live any more. I got my own ideas on how to raise
children."

"Well, have you got any ideas on how to raise eighty
dollars?"

Mom was silent.

"I thought you didn't. I'm going to have to work my
head off to get that money. But first I'm going to take it out
of your hides. You first, Roosevelt."

It didn't hurt so bad when he beat me and Cephas.
What hurt was hearing him threaten to beat Mom too. He
told her if she wanted to be in the country so bad, she
should go and find her a country man.

We were half afraid she would do just that. But,
though she cried and moaned all night long, she didn't go
nowhere.

It rained for more than a week. We couldn't have
gone outdoors if we'd been allowed to.

Then there was a clear day. Cephas and I came home
from school and decided to fool around outside for a
while. We wandered around to the back of the building.

The little patch of grass had been trimmed, and the
broken branch had been sawed off the tree so neatly you

couldn't tell it had been there. There was a little wire fence around the tree and a bigger one around the grass. It looked neat and perfect and dead. Just like a graveyard. Only thing missing was tombstones.

Cephas spotted something. "Hey, Roosevelt! Look!" he cried.

I looked where his finger was pointing. Coming up around the base of the tree were some broad, wrinkled, light-green leaves.

My watermelon vines!

I guess maybe you never seen a watermelon vine, but it's one of the biggest plants in the world. It spreads out all over the place and travels anywhere there's space for it to go.

My vines are almost four feet long now. I water them every night in the hour between dark and curfew. And I tell them what I want them to do:

"First, crawl in Mrs. Broadnax's window and choke her.

"Then make it so people won't have to live high up in the sky any more. Make it so they can come down, and plant things, and walk around on the ground.

"Send your roots under this building, and crack the foundations, and make it come tumbling down."

When it happens, I'll be King of the Mountain, sitting on top of the ruins with a hunk of watermelon in each hand.

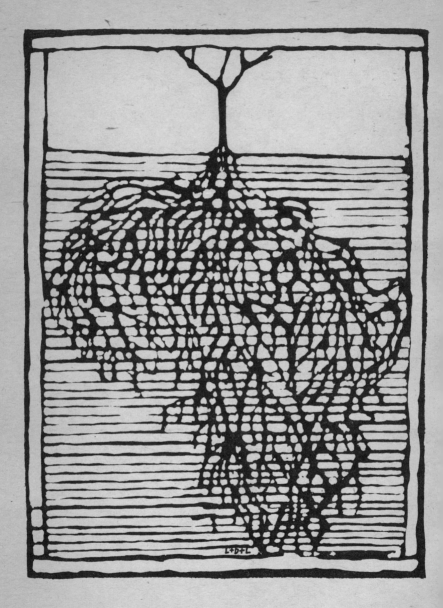

FEELINGS ABOUT MY ROOTS:
FOLKTALES
AND
FOLKWAYS

FROM *AFRICAN POEMS*

WE'RE an Africanpeople
hard-softness burning black.
the earth's magic color our veins.
an Africanpeople are we;
burning blacker softly, softer.

Don L. Lee

BROTHERS

We're related—you and I,
You from the West Indies,
I from Kentucky.

Kinsmen—you and I,
You from Africa,
I from the U.S.A.

Brothers—you and I.

Langston Hughes

THE SNAKE KING
retold by Kathleen Arnott

Temba had some friends who used to go into the forest every day to cut wood and bring it to sell in the market. Sometimes he went with them, for he was a splendid tree climber, and knew where the best firewood was to be found. He would hack the branches off with his cutlass and throw them to the ground and, in the way of all lads, he would sometimes boast, "See how much wood I have collected! I work much faster than you, my friends. Why don't you hurry more?"

Temba's friends often became angry with him, although they had to admit to themselves that he was a much stronger and faster worker than they were.

One day, after Temba had gathered a particularly large bundle of wood, he lay down under a tree to rest, and chided his companions good-naturedly, because he had already collected as much by himself as they had altogether. As he lay there, he began idly tapping the ground with a stone, beating it like a drummer.

Suddenly he sat up, tapped again, and called his friends to come.

"Listen!" he said. "This ground is hollow."

Sure enough, as the lads stopped talking and listened

to Temba tapping with his stone, they heard the hollow sound that showed there was a cavity below.

"Let us dig, to see what we find," suggested one of them, and they set to work at once, digging with their cutlasses.

After some time they discovered a large hole in the ground, which was full of wild bees' honey. They dipped their fingers in the honey and sucked them clean. It was delicious.

"What a find!" said one of the lads. "Now we need not cut firewood to sell, for we can take calabashes of honey to the market and sell those instead."

Temba agreed, but whereas he had never asked for any part of the money they made from selling firewood, now he told them he must have a share of what was given them for the honey. At first the boys refused, saying he had enough riches in his compound already; but Temba, who wanted the money to give to his parents, insisted, and at last his companions agreed.

Day after day the boys dipped their calabashes into the pit, then took the honey to the market where they found plenty of eager customers. They carefully concealed the pit by covering it with leafy branches and moss each time they left it, so that none of the people who lived nearby knew where the honey came from.

The pit was surprisingly deep, and as the level of the honey dropped, they had to tie a rope around the waist of one of the boys and let him down to fill the calabashes. Then they all hauled together to pull him up.

One morning when it was almost empty Temba was lowered into the hole. He filled the calabashes and sent them up to his companions on the end of the rope.

"In another day or two we shall have to go back to our woodcutting, for there is scarcely any honey left now," Temba called.

The lads looked at one another, remembering how Temba had taunted them for being slower than he was. Then one of them whispered, "Let us leave him there. We can manage our woodcutting without him, and nobody will find him in this pit."

"I'm ready!" shouted Temba. "Pull me up."

There was no answer. Without a word the boys replaced the branches and moss, and tiptoed away from the edge of the pit, gradually leaving Temba's cries behind them in the forest.

"What shall we say to Temba's mother?" asked one of the boys, as they made their way along the bush path which led to the village.

"We must tell her that a lion leaped upon him and dragged him away before we could save him," replied another.

So the callous boys told Temba's mother this lie, and she believed them since she had no reason to do otherwise, for everyone knew that hungry lions would seize a man.

She wept and mourned for many days, while her daughters and her little adopted son did their best to comfort her.

Now when Temba had called to his friends a dozen or more times, he began to suspect that a trick was being played on him.

"They are sure to come back before sundown," he said to himself, "so I will sleep until then."

Great was his surprise when he awoke to find that it

was night and his companions had not returned. There was no way out of the pit, for the sides were steep and slippery, and the boys had taken the ropes away with them. Temba ate some honey, for there was still a little left in the pit, and then for the rest of the night he sat thinking how he could escape.

By now he was certain that the boys had left him there on purpose, and he guessed that it was chiefly because they were jealous of him that they had been so unkind.

For three days he struggled to make steps up the side of the pit, but it was quite impossible without tools of any kind, and he began to despair. Then the next day he saw a scorpion creep out of the wall, and when he had killed it he said, "Where did that creature come from? It could not have lived in the soil, so there must be some kind of passage along which it crawled."

Scraping furiously with his hands at the spot where the scorpion had first appeared, Temba soon uncovered what seemed to be a narrow passage. After a few hours' work, he found that it was indeed a way out of the pit, although where the passage would lead him he could not tell.

He began to crawl along on his hands and knees, but soon the tunnel grew bigger, and he was able to stand and walk upright. Suddenly he gave a cry of joy, for at the far end he could see a gleam of light, and he knew he would soon be out of his prison.

He began to run, singing with happiness, and at last he found himself in the fresh air and sunshine again, standing in the middle of a wide open space. There were no people to be seen and he did not recognize the place, but noticing a little path, he decided to follow it.

The country seemed strange to him, and he was surprised at the unusual flowers and shrubs he saw growing at the sides of the path. The trees, too, bore different fruits from those he was accustomed to, but still he met no people, so he could not ask where he was.

Then as he turned a corner he came upon a beautiful house, far bigger than any he had seen near his own village.

"Who lives here?" he thought and, going up to the door, he called out greetings in his own language.

No one answered, so he put his hand on the door to open it and noticed that it was made of gold.

"A golden door!" he exclaimed. "What rich person lives here?"

Looking closer, he saw that the door was fastened by a golden latch in which was fixed a silver peg, and in no time at all, Temba had opened the door and stepped inside.

Never had he seen such a sight before. He found himself in a large reception room, with scores of beautifully carved chairs and stools standing against the walls. At the far end of the room was one very large chair made of shining gold, and studded with pearls and precious stones; it made Temba gasp to look at them.

"Where can this be?" he said to himself, "and who lives here in such splendor?"

There was nobody to answer his questions, and although he stood in the center of the reception room for some time, nobody came to ask him what he was doing there, and not a sound could be heard from any part of the big house.

At last Temba, who had not slept well during his

uncomfortable nights in the honey pit, could not keep his eyes open any longer. He caught sight of a long low chair in one corner, and soon he was stretched out upon it and had fallen fast asleep.

Some time later he awoke to hear voices outside, and before he could rouse himself sufficiently to get to his feet, he saw the strangest procession coming into the room.

First came some big gray snakes dressed as soldiers. Next came snakes with green and yellow markings on their backs, and last of all came one huge snake, gliding along in a most dignified way, dressed in beautiful silk robes with a golden crown on his head.

Temba rose to his feet and faced the crowd of snakes, although his heart was beating furiously.

"Who are you, and what are you doing in my house?" asked the magnificently dressed snake. "How dare you come into my palace like this without an invitation? Do you not know that I am King of the Snakes?"

When Temba heard this, he bowed low and told the King all that had happened to him since he had gone down into the pit to collect honey.

The soldier snakes closed in upon him and wanted to seize him, but the Snake King, looking into Temba's face and believing that he had told the truth, said to them, "Leave him alone. He is not an enemy. He shall be my guest."

Then the King sent his servants, those snakes which were green and yellow, to fetch food for Temba. They brought him delicious fruits such as he had never tasted before and clear cool water in a silver cup.

While he ate, he told the Snake King about his village, his parents, his sisters, and his little adopted brother. He explained that he was afraid his mother would be worrying because he had not returned from the forest.

The Snake King was sympathetic.

"Spend the night in my palace," he said, "and in the morning my soldiers will escort you to the borders of your own country. You would never find your way alone."

That night Temba slept on a soft bed, covered with a richly embroidered sleeping cloth, in the big reception room.

He was awakened by a snake servant bringing him a tray with delicious food on it, and when he had eaten, the Snake King came to see him.

"It has been good to have you here," said the King. "Men are the enemies of snakes, but you have not tried to harm any of my subjects and I am grateful to you. I will send you home now, but before you go, will you promise that whatever happens you will never harm me?"

"Of course I would not hurt you in any way," protested Temba. "Why should I, after the kindness you have shown?"

"Time will show," said the Snake King solemnly.

Then he gave his orders to a group of soldier snakes who led Temba from the palace along the little path he had followed the day before.

The journey was a long one. They went over a high hill, down into a deep valley, across a wide river by canoe, and through a dark forest. But at last Temba began to recognize some of the flowers which grew beside the path as those which bloomed near his own village, and then he knew he was getting back to the kingdom of men again.

The snakes stopped at a stream.

"Cross this water and you will be back in your own

land," said the leader. "Follow that stony path by the baobab tree, and it will take you to your home."

Temba thanked them courteously, crossed the stream, and soon arrived at the compound where his mother and family lived.

"Mother! Father!" he called in a loud voice as he went through the opening in the fence which surrounded their huts.

His mother, who was preparing the supper, dropped everything and ran toward him.

"My son! My son!" she cried. "They told me you had been killed by a lion! How did you escape?"

"It was all a mistake," replied Temba, not wishing to give his companions away. "After supper I will tell you my story."

When all Temba's family had greeted him, they sat on the ground to have supper outside their hut in the moonlight.

Then Temba told them that he had accidentally fallen into a pit, and they listened wide-eyed to his account of the Snake King and his kingdom.

The next day his companions came to him, and, falling on their knees, begged his forgiveness, promising that they would never do such a thing again.

Temba told them not to worry since they had been the means of giving him a most exciting adventure, which he then recounted to them. They were amazed and went back to their homes to tell the story to their families, so that everyone in the village knew that Temba had been the guest of the Snake King.

A week or two later, the Chief of that part of Africa became ill. Nothing his wise men and doctors could do made him better, and at last one very old, very wise man said to the others, "I have seen this sickness before. Our Chief will die unless we can obtain what is probably unobtainable—the heart of the King of the Snakes."

All the people were in despair, for no one knew where the King of the Snakes lived. But as the news of what was needed spread around the nearby villages, a friend of Temba's heard it and went running at once to the wise men.

"I can tell you who knows where the King of the Snakes lives!" he exclaimed triumphantly. "A boy called Temba visited the place a few weeks ago and came back to our village and told us about it."

The wise men were delighted and sent for Temba immediately, but when he heard that they wanted to kill the King of the Snakes and to use his heart for medicine, he would not tell them the way to the snakes' kingdom.

Then the wise men called the Chief's warriors, and they beat Temba, and tied his arms with ropes, and forced him to lead the way to the Snake King. Slowly and sadly he took them across the stream, through the forest, over the wide river in a canoe, down through the valley, over the hill, and at last he pointed out the King's palace to them.

They dragged and pushed him along in front of them, until they met a group of soldier snakes. Then a fierce battle began, and because the warriors were stronger and better armed, they soon drove all the soldier snakes into the bush and forced their way into the palace.

The Snake King was waiting on his bejeweled throne. The warriors rushed at him and bound him with rope and vines.

"Forgive me," whispered Temba. "I was forced to show them the way."

"I know," replied the Snake King softly. "But never fear. After they have killed me and taken my heart, throw my body into the stream that divides your country from ours, and all will be well."

He had just finished speaking when one of the warriors lifted his spear and plunged it into the King's side so that he died at once.

Then it was only a matter of moments before the heart had been cut out and placed in a bag around the warrior's neck, and the remains of the Snake King were left lying on the ground at Temba's feet.

The warriors departed swiftly, singing and shouting with joy, because they now had the medicine which would cure their Chief and they hoped for a big reward. They scarcely seemed to notice that Temba had been left behind, with his arms still bound.

After a long struggle he managed to free himself, and then sadly he picked up the body of his friend the Snake King, wrapped it in a cloth he found on a chair nearby, and began his long journey home.

It was almost dark when he reached the little stream. In the distance, on the other side, he could hear drumming and singing and general rejoicing, so he guessed that the Chief had recovered.

He paused and tried to remember exactly what the Snake King had said to him. Then he unwrapped the body, stood up, and threw it into the stream, where it sank to the bottom with a loud splash.

Temba waited, but nothing seemed to happen. It grew darker and the grasses behind him rustled, but he could not go home until he knew whether the King of the Snakes was alive again.

"Alas!" he said aloud. "What has happened to my friend? Is this the river he told me to throw him into, or have I made a mistake?"

"This is the river," said a voice behind him, and out of the darkness, gliding through the grass, came the Snake King.

"Thank you! You have brought me back to life," he said. "I shall return to my kingdom now, but never tell anyone in your village that I am alive again or they may seek me out a second time, if their Chief becomes ill."

"Good-by! I promise never to speak of it," replied Temba.

Then, watching until the Snake King disappeared into the darkness, he crossed the stream and went to his own village, where he joined in the dancing and singing with a light heart, knowing that his friend was alive and safe.

OL-AMBU AND HE-OF-THE-LONG-SLEEPING-PLACE

Verna Aardema

In a Masai kraal near the Kapiti Plains, there once lived a man who was brave and strong and clever. But he talked so much about himself that he came to be called Ol-Ambu, the boaster.

One morning when the sky was red from the rising sun, Ol-Ambu dipped some arrows in poison. He wrapped the tips in a strip of hide, licking the end to make it stick. Then he put the arrows into his pouch, picked up his bow, and set out on a hunt.

Ol-Ambu followed a path that led to the grassland. Where the forest ended and the plains spread out before him, he stopped. He looked over the sea of brown grass with acacia trees and thornbushes scattered over it. And his eyes fell upon the largest giraffe he had ever seen.

With his tongue, the animal was plucking the tender leaves and soft thorns from the tips of the top branches of a small acacia tree. He was taller than two huts, one above the other. Ol-Ambu knew at once that it was O-ado-kiragata, He-of-the-Long-Sleeping-Place.

Ol-Ambu drew in his breath as he thought of the

story it would make—how he, Ol-Ambu, all by himself, had killed He-of-the-Long-Sleeping-Place.

But as he pondered about how to do it, he remembered that many men had tried to get the big giraffe, and had failed. He said to himself, "One man is not enough. However brave a man may be, two brave men are better."

Then quietly he turned back down the path toward the village to get someone to help him. On the way he met his friend Pambito. He asked Pambito to help him get the big giraffe. Pambito was glad to take part in anything so exciting. So the two hurried back to the grassy plain.

When they arrived, they saw that He-of-the-Long-Sleeping-Place was gone. The two men studied the tracks around the nearest acacia trees. And under the largest tree, on the side where the shade was densest, Ol-Ambu saw a much-trampled place. "Ho!" he said, "look here! This is where O-ado-kiragata stands to rest at midday. He has probably gone to a water hole to drink now. But the sun is almost opposite. He will come back. This is the only tree around tall enough to shade him."

Then Ol-Ambu thought of a plan. "Give me your knife, Pambito," he said. "You take my bow and arrows. I'll climb the tree above the giraffe's shady place. When he comes, I'll drop onto his back and stab him in the neck. You hide behind those bushes. When I fall upon him, you shoot him. If the knife fails to kill him, the poison arrow will."

The men traded weapons. Ol-Ambu climbed the tree, and Pambito hid behind the bushes. After a while, He-of-the-Long-Sleeping-Place returned. And just as Ol-Ambu had guessed, he came to stand in the shadiest spot under the big acacia tree.

Pambito unwrapped the arrows, strung one to the bow, and crouched, ready to leap up and shoot at the proper moment. Ol-Ambu waited until the head of the giraffe drooped in sleep. Then he dropped astraddle his back, threw his arms around the huge neck, and yelled, "Aiya! Aiya!"

O-ado-kiragata reared up onto his hind legs and tossed his long neck one way, then the other. Ol-Ambu was thrown to one side, and he found himself dangling from the giraffe's neck like a baby monkey clinging to its mother.

The big giraffe then stretched out into a fast gallop. Now Pambito, on hearing Ol-Ambu's cry, leaped up to let the arrow fly. But when he saw Ol-Ambu dangling from the neck of the galloping giraffe, he laughed so hard that he couldn't shoot at all! He laughed and laughed until he fell over in a fit.

Ol-Ambu heard Pambito roaring with laughter. But *he* didn't laugh! He hung onto the neck of the giraffe for his life! He knew that if he fell, a kick from one of those powerful feet would finish him. Finally he drew himself up and managed to straddle the long, sloping back. The giraffe carried him far. But, at last, Ol-Ambu was able to draw his knife and stab him in the neck. Then the animal fell, struggled a little, and died.

Ol-Ambu cut out some of the fat and set out with it to find Pambito. When he came back to the big acacia tree, he found his friend lying unconscious. He said to himself, "Pambito likes fat. Nothing will arouse him quicker than freshly roasted fat."

He took out his fire stick, made a small fire, and roasted the fat. Then he passed it back and forth under

Pambito's nose. The man stirred, opened his eyes, and said, "Yee! So you got him! Give me some of that meat!"

Pambito went with Ol-Ambu back to the giraffe to help him skin it. When they had finished, they built a fire and roasted some meat. As they ate together, Ol-Ambu said, "I have been thinking. Why should I give you half of this meat? You just laughed when you should have been helping. You laughed when my very life was in danger. For helping with the skinning, you have already been paid with this meal. Now go and leave me."

Pambito went back to the kraal, and walked past Ol-Ambu's hut. Enoti, Ol-Ambu's wife, came out. "Have you seen Ol-Ambu?" she asked.

"No," Pambito lied. "But I heard that he has killed a giraffe. I also heard that he is very angry with you, and when he comes home he is going to beat you."

"Why should be want to beat me?" asked Enoti. "I have done nothing!" After Pambito was gone, she thought it might be wise for her to go to visit a friend on the far side of the kraal until Ol-Ambu's anger cooled.

Now, Pambito was watching from a little distance. When he saw Enoti leave, he entered her house.

The next morning, Ol-Ambu returned with the first load of meat. He did not come to the door, but called through a hole in the wall at the back of the hut. Pambito, changing his voice so that it sounded like Enoti's, answered. When Ol-Ambu was satisfied that his wife was there, he called: "Take the meat as I pass it to you through the hole. Prepare it, and tonight we shall have a feast for the whole kraal. Then I shall tell how, all by myself, I killed O-ado-kiragata."

Ol-Ambu, thinking his meat was in safe hands, went

back to the place where he had killed the giraffe, to fetch another load. While he was gone, Pambito carried the meat off to his own hut, and told his wife to start preparing it for a feast. Then he returned to Ol-Ambu's hut to wait for the rest. When several loads had thus been brought by Ol-Ambu, Pambito decided there couldn't be much left. So he went off to find Enoti. As he expected, she was at the house of her friend.

"Enoti," said Pambito, "did you really believe me when I told you Ol-Ambu was going to beat you? I was only joking! But he should be getting back with that giraffe meat any time now. You'd better get home before he returns, or he really will be angry with you!"

Enoti hurried home. Soon Ol-Ambu arrived with a load of meat wrapped in a piece of the hide. He put down the bundle, and handed Enoti a handful of the long black hairs from the giraffe's tail.

"Eiji!" cried Enoti. "Sewing thread. Thank you." Then she hurried to fetch Ol-Ambu's stool and his snuff, for she knew he must be tired.

Ol-Ambu sat down and stretched out his feet. Enoti looked at the bundle of meat. "Is that all the meat?" she asked.

Ol-Ambu said, "That's all of it."

"It must have been a very small giraffe," said Enoti.

"Small!" cried Ol-Ambu. "Didn't I tell you this morning it was O-ado-kiragata himself? Where is the rest of it?"

"The rest of what!" cried Enoti.

Ol-Ambu said, "The whole giraffe that I brought home."

"I haven't seen it," said Enoti. "I haven't even been home."

Ol-Ambu was about to beat her, for he thought she was lying.

Then the whole affair became clear to Enoti, and she said, "It was Pambito who stole the giraffe meat. His wife is cooking it now out in the plaza."

Then Ol-Ambu covered his face. He realized that he had lost almost the whole giraffe and that Pambito had made a fool of him, all because he had refused to share.

ANCESTORS

Why are our ancestors
always kings and princes
and never the common people?

Was the Old Country a democracy
where every man was a king?
Or did the slave-catchers
steal only the aristocrats
and leave the fieldhands
laborers
street cleaners
garbage collectors
dish washers
cooks
and maids
behind?

My own ancestor
(research reveals)
was a swineherd
who tended the pigs
in the Royal Pigstye
and slept in the mud
among the hogs.

Yet I'm as proud of him
as of any king or prince
dreamed up in fantasies
of bygone glory.

Dudley Randall

FEELING THE PAIN
AND PRIDE
OF STRUGGLE

MY PEOPLE

The night is beautiful,
So the faces of my people.

The stars are beautiful,
So the eyes of my people.

Beautiful, also, is the sun.
Beautiful, also, are the souls of my people.

Langston Hughes

MY PA
WAS NEVER SLAVE

Slave?
My pa was never slave.
And those
Who thought   they made him   slave, didn't
Understand
The word.
He saw beyond the cottonfields and
Cornfields
That blinded
Their eyes;
Beyond the valleys, dark with their sins, the sunrise,
They
Could not conceive. This,
                    Pa knew.
                        This,   I know.

Harriet Wheatley

WHEN THE RATTLESNAKE SOUNDS
A play by *Alice Childress*

Harriet Tubman was born the slave of Edward Brodas in Mary-
land about 1821. She died March 10, 1913, in Auburn, New
York. She fully felt the indignities and cruelty of slavery, suffer-
ing beatings, injuries and working as a field hand under subhu-
man conditions. When she reached womanhood, she dreamed
of running North to free territory. She took others with her
when she went, then returned many times to rescue more than
three hundred black men, women, and children . . . by way of
the Underground Railroad, a route made up of secret paths and
hiding places in the homes of those who wanted slavery abol-
ished. She spent her life as an Underground Conductor and
also earned money to contribute to the funds raised by abolitionists for food, medicine, clothing, etc. needed for the rescue
work. One summer she worked as a laundress in a hotel at Cape
May, New Jersey. This fact inspired the author to write the
following play which is fictional but based upon Harriet Tubman's true feelings, as expressed by her many times, concerning
commitment and fear.

CHARACTERS

HARRIET TUBMAN: *An experienced leader who knows how to handle people with firmness . . . and love. Actually she was a little woman, five feet tall, but for the purposes of a play the qualities of leadership and compassion are more important than actual appearance. She is in her early forties.*

LENNIE: *A strong, determined, no-nonsense kind of young woman. She is used to hard work and is perhaps physically stronger than* HARRIET, *but does not have the tact to handle leadership. She is about twenty-five years old.*

CELIA: *A very attractive young woman who has certainly been more sheltered than the other two.* CELIA *is also a dedicated person . . . but she sees the freedom struggle in romantic terms . . . and has the tendency to get fed up when the going is grubby and ordinary.*

TIME: *Very close to the end of legal slavery.*

PLACE: *Cape May, New Jersey.*

SCENE: *A hotel laundry room.*

*There is a pile of loose laundry on the floor waiting to be done . . .
much with flounces and lace to suggest the summer clothing of
ladies in the 1860s. There are three washtubs filled with water
and laundry; in each tub is a washboard.* HARRIET, LENNIE, *and*
CELIA *are washing clothes. The women are dressed in calico
dresses and aprons.* HARRIET *and* LENNIE *work vigorously,
absorbed in the task.* CELIA *is slowing up and finally stops.*

CELIA (*cautiously watching* HARRIET *and* LENNIE) Lord, I'm
tired. (*Others keep working.*) Seem like we workin way
past our dinnertime, don't it? Harriet? Lennie?

LENNIE Not much past dinner. It feels like about one
o'clock.

HARRIET We're gonna stop an eat by 'n by. We'll put out
five bundles of wash today. Yesterday was only four.

CELIA *Only* four? When I went to bed last night, I cried, I
was so bone-weary. Only? How can four bundles of
wash be *only*?

HARRIET Just a while longer, Celia. Let's sing. When you
singin, the work goes fast. You pick a song, Lennie.

LENNIE (*decides to pick one that will annoy* CELIA) Wadin in

the water, wadin in the water (children) Wadin in the
water, God gonna trouble the water.
(HARRIET *joins her in singing.*)

CELIA   (*drying her hands on her apron*)   I want my dinner
now. I'm hungry.

LENNIE   We all hungry, Celia. Can't you hold out a little
more?

CELIA   If we *all* hungry, why don't we *all* eat? We been up
since seven this mornin . . . workin. For what? Why?

LENNIE   You know why! We got to finish five bundles.

CELIA   (*to the heavens above*)   Five bundles for what?

LENNIE   For a dollar and a quarter, that's what! (*Grum-
bling*) I'm tellin you . . . some people.

HARRIET   (*Sensing trouble, she stops washing.*)   Celia is right,
Lennie. It's not good to kill yourself workin.

LENNIE   (*in anger*)   She knows why we're doin it, Harriet. Some people . . . I'm tellin you.

HARRIET   (*firmly*)   Let's have our dinner, Lennie.

LENNIE   (*her eyes on* CELIA)   Did you fix it again, Harriet?
We suppose to take turns. I take a turn, you take a turn,
then . . .

HARRIET (*hastily cutting her off*) I got some nice corn bread and some side meat. The coffee should be ready. (*Handing out paper parcels to the girls*) We need to rest awhile. Here, Celia, and that's yours, Lennie. (*Going back to her tub*) I'll just wash out these few more pieces before my water turns cold.

LENNIE I ain't restin unless you rest too. Not like some people I know.

CELIA She keep sayin *some people*. Wonder who she means?

HARRIET (*with a sigh*) I'll stop too.

CELIA (*looking at the pile of unwashed clothes as she unwraps her lunch*) White folks love white clothes and they love to sit in the grass too . . . and I'm sick of scrubbin grass stains.

HARRIET Well, we need the money.

CELIA (*puts down her lunch and snatches up a flouncy white dress*) Look at all the money *they* got. This cost every bit of twelve dollars. (*Imitating the hotel guests*) Spendin the summer in a big hotel, ridin round in carriages. (*Drops her airy act and goes back to anger*) If just one of em give us what she spend in a week . . . we wouldn't have to work two months in no hotel laundry.

LENNIE I got a life-size picture of them givin you that

much money. They ain't gonna give you nothin, so you better be glad you got the chance to *earn* some.

CELIA Scrubbin! Ain't that a damn somethin to be glad about? Excuse me, Harriet, I meant to say dern or drat.

HARRIET Celia got somethin on her mind, and she need to talk, so let her talk, Lennie. But no dammin, dernin, or drattin either. All here got more manners than to cuss.

LENNIE (*as she looks at* HARRIET'S *food*) Is that your dinner? You ain't got no meat on your bread, Harriet.

HARRIET I don't too much like meat.

LENNIE I know who do. Some people.

CELIA (*bursting out at* HARRIET) Stop sayin that! You do too like meat! Stop makin out like you don't. You goin without so you can save another nickel. Yall drivin me outta my head. Maybe I'm just not suited for this kinda thing.

LENNIE But I am, huh?

HARRIET (*quietly and seriously*) You tired of this bargain we made? You sorry about it and don't know how to quit?

LENNIE (*flaring with anger*) She promised and she got to stick by it! Your father is a *deacon of the church* . . . and if

you don't keep your word, you gonna bring disgrace
down on him and *every member* of your family.

HARRIET   Lennie, don't be so brash. Mother and father is
one thing . . . child is another. Each one stands upon
his own deeds. She don't have to stay. Celia, you can go
if you want.

CELIA   I don't really want to get out of it. But I want *some*
of my money for myself. I'm tired of sleepin three in a
room. I want to spend a little of the money . . . just a
little, Harriet. Buy a few treats.

LENNIE   She's jealous of them rich white ladies . . . cause
they got silk parasols to match they dresses. I heard her
say it. "Wish I had me a silk parasol."

HARRIET   We eatin and sleepin. We spend for that and
nothin more . . . that was the bargain.

CELIA   (*to* LENNIE)   I could own a silk parasol *and* carry it
. . . without actin like a field hand.

HARRIET   I been a field hand, children. Harness to a plow
like a workhorse.

CELIA   Scuse me, I'm sorry.

LENNIE   (*really sarcastic*)   Celia, that don't sound nothin
like them big speeches you used to make in church
meetin. (*Mocking* CELIA) "I'll die for my freedom!" . . .
Had everybody whoopin and hollerin every time you

open your mouth, whole church stompin and shoutin amen.

CELIA (*sadly*) I remember how it was.

(*The women remove their aprons and* HARRIET *takes her place center stage. Church music in from offstage tape or recording of "The Old Ship of Zion," or any of the A. M. E. Zion songs.* HARRIET TUBMAN *was a member of that church. She addresses the audience as though they are the congregation.*)

HARRIET (*Music and humming are in low as she speaks.*) God bless you, brothers and sisters, bless you, children.

OFFSTAGE VOICES PLUS LENNIE AND CELIA   Amen . . . Amen . . . Bless God.

HARRIET I thank the good Lord for the support of the African Methodist Episcopal Zion Church in the freedom struggle. There is comfort and good fellowship here.

CHURCH VOICES Yes, Lord. Amen.

HARRIET Not like hidin in the bitter cold, with the huntin dogs followin you down with no restin place in sight. We had to give the little babies paregoric so they wouldn't cry and let the paddy-rollers know where to find us. We crossed some lonely roads and rivers . . . the dark of the night around us, the clouds cuttin off the sight of the North Star. But everything was all right

cause where I go . . . God goes . . . and I carry a gun
. . . two guns . . . a hand pistol and a shoulder rifle
. . . just in case the Lord tell me I got to use it!

CHURCH VOICES   Amen! Speak! Praise the holy name!
Amen!

HARRIET   I thank the Father for the help and assistance of
the Society of Friends, and the abolitionists, and all well-
wishers.

CHURCH VOICES   Amen, Amen, Amen.

HARRIET   But as I put my hand to the plow to do the work
of Freedom, so I also put *my money* into the work. I have
none now, so I will spend my summer washin and
ironin so that when the fall come I have *some of my own*
to put . . . to buy food, medicine, paregoric for the
babies, and ammunition for the pistol. . . . Lord grant I
never use it. Any ladies here want to go with me to
wash clothes and give the money to free our slave
brethren?

LENNIE   (*stands by* HARRIET's *side*)   If you would have me,
Mrs. Tubman, it would be the greatest honor, a great
honor indeed.

HARRIET   Thank you, my daughter.

CELIA   (*stands up and throws her arms out in a Joan of Arc
gesture*)   I'll die for my freedom! Take me, Sister! I'm
ready to fight the good fight. Hallelujah!

CHURCH VOICES   (CELIA *has set the church to rocking.*)
Glory! Glory! Hallelujah! Fight the good fight! Amen!
(*Music fades out as women don their aprons again.*)

CELIA   I remember how it was, Lennie, and the promise I
made. But how much can we get like this? Maybe if
everybody worked and gave their money to the Underground, it would mean somethin. This way I just can't
see it, but I believe in freedom and I understand.

HARRIET   Ain't no such thing as only "understandin."
Understandin mean action. You have to look after what
Celia does . . . and if *nobody else* do nothin, you got to.
Freedom is just a baby, and you its mother. You don't
stop lovin and carin for it just cause others don't care.

CELIA   Maybe it's easy to talk like that when you Moses.
It's easy to kill yourself for somethin when thousands of
people be cheerin you on. Lennie and Celia don't mean
nothin to nobody. We could die here and nobody would
know or care.

LENNIE   Don't you talk for me! Ain't nothin greater to me
than to be able to say . . . "I, Lennie Brown, scrubbed
clothes side by side with Moses." If you lookin for
praise, you don't belong here.

HARRIET   Children, let us keep peace. We act like we hate
each other worse than we hate the slaveowner.

CELIA   I know what I sound like. . . . (*Falls at* HARRIET's
feet and holds out her hands) Oh, Harriet, my hands are

skinned sore.

LENNIE   Do, Jesus, look at Celia's hands.

HARRIET   (*turns* CELIA'S *head and searches for the truth*)   But it ain't your hands that's really botherin you. It ain't food, it ain't sleepin three in a room, and it ain't about silk parasols. What's botherin you, Celia?

CELIA   I'm so shame for feelin the way I do. Lord knows I'm shame.

HARRIET   Tell it. Speak your shame.

CELIA   I'm *scared*. If these people in this hotel knew who you was. Forty thousand dollars' reward out for you!

LENNIE   (*dashes to the door to see if anyone is around to listen*)   Hush your fool mouth! Moses got the charm. Slave holder will never catch Moses.

CELIA   I'm so shame. All those other things just lies. I ain't so terrible tired. I'm just scared and shame cause I'm afraid. Me talkin so big. Sure, I'd work all summer and give the money to the Underground. It did sound so good in the meetin where it was all warm and friendly. Now I'm scared of gettin into trouble. I never been no slave. And I'm scared of nothin round me but white folks.

LENNIE   We ain't got no room for no rabbity, timid kinda women in this work.

HARRIET Oh, yes, Lennie, we got room for the timid and the brave. Poor little Celia. Child, you lookin at a woman who's been plenty afraid. When the rattlesnake sounds a warnin . . . it's time to be scared. Ain't that natural? When I run away was nobody to cheer me on . . . don't you think I was scared?

LENNIE But you got to freedom.

HARRIET (*The feeling of a "meeting" begins.*) Oh, but when I found I'd crossed that line! There was such a glory over everything. The sun came shinin like gold through the trees.

LENNIE (*feels she is at church meeting*) You felt like you was in heaven! You was free!

HARRIET But there was no one to welcome me in the land of freedom. I was a stranger in a strange land. My home, after all, was down in the old cabin quarters with the ones I knew and loved . . . my slave mother and father, brothers, sisters and friends. Aunt Day . . . she used to be midwife, tend the sick, bury the dead. Two field hands I knew, they used to ease some the work off the women who was expectin. There I was standin on free land, with my heart back down there with them. What good is freedom without your people?

LENNIE Go on, Harriet!

HARRIET And so to this solemn resolution I come: As I was free . . . *they* would be free also.

LENNIE   Praise God, that's Harriet Tubman!

HARRIET   Sometimes I was scared in the icy river. Chilled to the bone and just might drown.

LENNIE   But you got cross.

HARRIET   I was scared in the dark and the swamp . . . but I come to the light. Most times I was full of hatred for the white folks.

LENNIE   And you came to the Friends.

HARRIET   And I came to John Brown.
(*Offstage music . . . soft violin . . . sound of voices ad-libbing at a reception*)
There was this big, fine affair, a reception. Abolitionist reception. The ladies were all dressed in lovely gowns, made by free labor. I was in my best too . . . but that wasn't too much better than what I'm standin in. They had pretty cakes and a punch bowl . . . the grandest party. Violin music . . . what you call elegant. There was a goodly crowd, and I was way on the other side of the room, away from the main door where the people would enter. Everybody called him Captain Brown . . . Captain.

(HARRIET *moves to the far side of the stage and turns toward the opposite door to illustrate the distance between her and Captain Brown.*)

HARRIET   The whisper started way down the hall and came through the room . . . "It's Captain Brown. He's here. Captain Brown is about to enter." Then he came in the door. He was a fine, stern-lookin gentleman . . . goodness glowed from his face like a burnin light. The room got quiet. He looked all around until he saw me. Mind now, we had never met. The ladies and gentlemen were all tryin to meet him. . . . Oh, it was Captain, Captain, Captain. He held up his hand. There was silence, then he said . . . "The first I see is General Tubman. The second is General Tubman. The third is General Tubman." He crossed the room and bowed to me . . . and I shook his hand.

LENNIE   And he died for us, didn't he?

HARRIET   Celia, he was a brave man, but I believe he must have been scared sometimes. But he did what he had to do.

CELIA   I guess he was just brave. Some folks braver than others.

HARRIET   I was with hundreds of brave black men on battleground. I was there, Celia. We saw the lightning and that was the guns, then we heard the thunder and that was the big guns, then we heard the rain falling. . . . And that was the drops of blood. And when we came to get the crops, it was dead men we reaped.

LENNIE   Fightin for us to be free. I guess they musta been scared sometimes.

HARRIET   Give me your hand, Celia. Look, see the skin

broken across the knuckles. Counta you some man or woman gonna have warm socks and boots to help em get to freedom. See the cuts the lye soap put in your skin. Counta you some little baby is gonna be born on free soil. It won't matter to him that you was afraid, won't matter that he did not know your name. Won't nothin count ceptin he's free. A livin monument to Celia's work.

(CELIA *cries*.)

You go to the room and rest. Maybe you might want to stay here after you think about it.

LENNIE   Sure, Celia . . . think about it. We can manage. And if you want to go home, we won't hold it against you. I ought not to have said what I did. Sometimes I get scared myself . . . but it makes me act evil *and* brave, you know?

CELIA   I don't want to go home. Guess there's worse things than fear. I'm glad to know I don't have to be shame about it.

HARRIET   That's right. If you was home doin nothin, what would you have to be fraid bout? That's when a woman oughta feel shame, shame to her very soul.

CELIA   (*Gathers up clothes, places them in tub, starts working.* HARRIET *goes to her tub.*) If we sing, the work goes faster.

LENNIE   (*goes to her tub*)   Your time to pick a song, Celia.

CELIA   (CELIA *starts scrubbing. They all work for a few mo-*
ments. CELIA *has decided on a song. She sings out.*)
Oh, Lord, I don't feel no ways tired
Children, Oh, Glory Hallelujah
For I hope to shout *Glory* when this world
   is all on fire
Oh, Glory, Hallelujah
   (*The others join her on the second round.*)
Oh, Lord, I don't feel no ways tired. . . .

CURTAIN

FROM *ROSA PARKS*

Eloise Greenfield

Rosa Parks' fight against discrimination began in Montgomery, Alabama, in 1955. At that time, there were laws throughout the South, known as Jim Crow laws, that discriminated against blacks. In Montgomery, there were specific laws that said that a black person was only allowed to ride in the back section of a public bus.

Rosa Parks' refusal to give up her seat began a protest that changed history. The peaceful protest organized by the Montgomery Improvement Association led the way for civil rights actions all over the South. And on December 13, 1956, as a result of the court cases and protests that began with Rosa Parks, the United States Supreme Court ruled that the law requiring segregation on public buses was unconstitutional.

—D.S.S.

On Thursday evening, December 1, 1955, Rosa left work and started home. She was tired. Her shoulders ached from bending over the sewing machine all day. "Today, I'll ride the bus," she thought.

She got on and sat in the first seat for blacks, right behind the white section. After a few stops the seats were filled. A white man got on. He looked for an empty seat. Then he looked at the driver. The driver came over to Rosa.

"You have to get up," he said.

All of a sudden Rosa knew she was not going to give up her seat. It was not fair. She had paid her money just as the man had. This time she was not going to move.

"No," she said softly.

"You'd better get up, or I'll call the police," the driver said.

It was very quiet on the bus now. Everyone stopped talking and watched. Still, Rosa did not move.

"Are you going to get up?"

"No," she repeated.

The driver left the bus and returned with two policemen.

"You're under arrest," they told her.

Rosa walked off the bus. The policemen put her in their car and drove to the police station. One policeman stuck a camera in her face and took her picture. Another took her fingerprints. Then she was locked in a cell.

Rosa felt very bad, sitting in that little room with iron bars. But she did not cry. She was a religious woman, and she thought of her faith in God. She said a silent prayer. Then she waited.

Someone who had seen Rosa arrested called Edgar Daniel Nixon of the NAACP. Mr. Nixon went right away to the police station and posted a hundred dollar bond for Rosa. This meant that she could leave, but that she promised to go to court on Monday for her trial.

Rosa left the police station. She had been locked up for two and a half hours. Mr. Nixon drove her home. At her apartment Rosa, her husband, Mr. Nixon, and Fred Gray, a lawyer, talked about what had happened. They thought they saw a way to solve the problem of the buses.

Mr. Gray would go into court with Rosa. He would prove that the bus company was not obeying the United States Constitution. The Constitution is an important paper that was written by the men who started the United States. It says that all the citizens of the United States must be treated fairly.

The next morning Rosa went to her job as usual. Her employer was surprised to see her. He had read about her arrest in the newspaper, and he thought she would be too upset to come in. Some of the white workers gave Rosa mean looks and would not speak to her. But she went on with her work.

That night Rosa met with a group of ministers and other black leaders of the city. Dr. Martin Luther King was one of the ministers. The black men and women of Montgomery were angry again. But this time they knew what to do.

"If the bus company won't treat us courteously," one

leader said, "we won't spend our money to ride the buses. We'll walk!"

After the meeting some of the people printed little sheets of paper. These sheets of paper, called leaflets, said, "DON'T RIDE THE BUS TO WORK, TO TOWN, TO SCHOOL, OR ANYWHERE, MONDAY, DECEMBER 5." They also invited people to a church meeting on Monday night. The leaflets were left everywhere—in mail boxes, on porches, in drugstores.

On Sunday morning black ministers all over the city preached about Rosa in their churches. Dr. King preached from his pulpit at the Dexter Avenue Baptist Church.

The preachers said, "Brothers and sisters, if you don't like what happened to Rosa Parks and what has been happening to us all these years, do something about it. Walk!"

And the people said, "Amen. We'll walk."

On Monday morning, no one was riding the buses. There were many people on the street, but everyone was walking. They were cheering because the buses were empty.

Rosa got up early that morning. She went to court with her lawyer for her trial. The judge found her guilty. But she and her lawyer did not agree with him. Her lawyer said, "We'll get a higher court to decide. If we have to, we'll take the case to the highest court in the United States."

That night thousands of people went to the church meeting. There were so many people that most of them had to stand outside and listen through a loudspeaker.

First there was prayer. Then Rosa Parks was introduced. She stood up slowly. The audience rose to its feet and clapped and cheered. After Rosa sat down, several ministers gave their speeches. Finally Dr. Martin Luther King started to speak.

"We are tired," he said.

"Yes, Lord," the crowd answered.

"We are tired of being kicked around," he said.

"Yes, Lord," they answered.

"We're not going to be kicked around anymore," Dr. King said. "We walked one day. Now we are going to have a real protest. We are going to keep walking until the bus company gives us fair treatment."

After Dr. King finished speaking, the Montgomery Improvement Association was formed to plan the protest. Dr. King was made president.

Then there was hymn singing and hand clapping. The people went home feeling good. All that walking was not going to be easy, but they knew they could do it.

I HAVE A DREAM

Martin Luther King, Jr.

On August 28, 1963, over 200,000 people gathered at the Washington Monument in Washington, D.C. Both black and white, they came from every part of the United States to express their belief in full equality for all Americans. Many speakers were heard that day; however none was more eagerly awaited or better remembered than Dr. Martin Luther King, Jr. His teachings on nonviolence had already made him a symbol of the struggle for civil rights in America. What follows is an excerpt from that speech.

—D.S.S.

I say to you today, my friends, even though we face the difficulties of today and tomorrow, I still have a dream. It is a dream deeply rooted in the American Dream. I have a dream that one day this nation will rise up and live out the true meaning of its creed: "We hold these truths to be self-evident, that all men are created equal."

I have a dream that one day on the red hills of Georgia the sons of former slaves and the sons of former slave-owners will be able to sit down together at the table of brotherhood.

I have a dream that one day even the state of Mississippi, a state sweltering with the heat of injustice and oppression, will be transformed into an oasis of freedom and justice.

I have a dream that my four little children will one day live in a nation where they will not be judged by the color of their skin but by the content of their character.

I have a dream today.

I have a dream that one day down in Alabama . . . little black boys and little black girls will be able to join hands with little white boys and white girls as sisters and brothers.

I have a dream today.

I have a dream that one day every valley shall be exalted, every hill and mountain shall be made low. The rough places will be made plain and the crooked places will be made straight. . . .

This is my hope and this is the faith with which I go back to the South. With this faith we will be able to hew out of the mountain of despair a stone of hope. . . . With this faith we will be able to work together, to pray together, to struggle together . . . to stand up for freedom together knowing that we will be free one day.

This will be the day when all of God's children will be able to sing with new meaning . . . "let freedom ring." Let freedom ring from the hilltops of New Hampshire. Let freedom ring from the mighty mountains of New York. Let freedom ring from the snow-capped Rockies of Colorado. But not only that, let freedom ring from Stone Mountain of Georgia and Lookout Mountain of Tennessee—from every hill and molehill and from every mountainside.

When we allow freedom to ring—when we let it ring from every village and every hamlet, from every state and every city, we will be able to speed up that day when all of God's children, black men and white men, Jews and gentiles, Protestants and Catholics, will be able to join hands and sing in the words of the Negro spiritual, "Free at last, Free at last, Thank God Almighty, we are free at last."

FEELINGS ABOUT
WHO I AM
AND
WHAT I WANT TO BE

LINEAGE

My grandmothers were strong.
They followed plows and bent to toil.
They moved through fields sowing seed.
They touched earth and grain grew.
They were full of sturdiness and singing.
My grandmothers were strong.

My grandmothers are full of memories
Smelling of soap and onions and wet clay
With veins rolling roughly over quick hands
They have many clean words to say.
My grandmothers were strong.
Why am I not as they?

Margaret Walker

KNOXVILLE, TENNESSEE

I always like summer
best
you can eat fresh corn
from daddy's garden
and okra
and greens
and cabbage
and lots of
barbecue
and buttermilk
and homemade ice cream
at the church picnic
and listen to
gospel music
outside
at the church
homecoming
and go to the mountains with
your grandmother
and go barefooted
and be warm
all the time
not only when you go to bed
and sleep

Nikki Giovanni

FROM *I KNOW WHY THE CAGED BIRD SINGS*

Maya Angelou

[In Stamps] I met, or rather got to know, the lady who threw me my first life line.

Mrs. Bertha Flowers was the aristocrat of Black Stamps. She had the grace of control to appear warm in the coldest weather, and on the Arkansas summer days it seemed she had a private breeze which swirled around, cooling her. She was thin without the taut look of wiry people, and her printed voile dresses and flowered hats were as right for her as denim overalls for a farmer. She was our side's answer to the richest white woman in town.

Her skin was a rich black that would have peeled like a plum if snagged, but then no one would have thought of getting close enough to Mrs. Flowers to ruffle her dress, let alone snag her skin. She didn't encourage familiarity. She wore gloves too.

I didn't think I ever saw Mrs. Flowers laugh, but she smiled often. A slow widening of her thin black lips to show even, small white teeth, then the slow effortless closing. When she chose to smile on me, I always wanted to thank her. The action was so graceful and inclusively benign.

She was one of the few gentlewomen I have ever known, and has remained throughout my life the measure of what a human being can be.

Momma had a strange relationship with her. Most often when she passed on the road in front of the Store, she spoke to Momma in that soft yet carrying voice, "Good day, Mrs. Henderson." Momma responded with "How you, Sister Flowers?"

Mrs. Flowers didn't belong to our church, nor was she Momma's familiar. Why on earth did she insist on calling her Sister Flowers? Shame made me want to hide my face. Mrs. Flowers deserved better than to be called Sister. Then, Momma left out the verb. Why not ask, "How *are* you, *Mrs.* Flowers?" With the unbalanced passion of the young, I hated her for showing her ignorance to Mrs. Flowers. It didn't occur to me for many years that they were as alike as sisters, separated only by formal education.

Although I was upset, neither of the women was in the least shaken by what I thought an unceremonious greeting. Mrs. Flowers would continue her easy gait up the hill to her little bungalow, and Momma kept on shelling peas or doing whatever had brought her to the front porch.

Occasionally, though, Mrs. Flowers would drift off the road and down to the Store and Momma would say to me, "Sister, you go on and play." As I left I would hear the beginning of an intimate conversation. Momma persistently using the wrong verb, or none at all.

"Brother and Sister Wilcox is sho'ly the meanest——"

"Is," Momma? "Is?" Oh, please, not "is," Momma, for two or more. But they talked, and from the side of the building where I waited for the ground to open up and swallow me, I heard the soft-voiced Mrs. Flowers and the textured voice of my grandmother merging and melting. They were interrupted from time to time by giggles that must have come from Mrs. Flowers (Momma never giggled in her life). Then she was gone.

She appealed to me because she was like people I had never met personally. Like women in English novels who walked the moors (whatever they were) with their loyal dogs racing at a respectful distance. Like the women who sat in front of roaring fireplaces, drinking tea incessantly from silver trays full of scones and crumpets. Women who walked over the "heath" and read morocco-bound books and had two last names divided by a hyphen. It would be safe to say that she made me proud to be Negro, just by being herself.

She acted just as refined as whitefolks in the movies and books and she was more beautiful, for none of them could have come near that warm color without looking gray by comparison.

It was fortunate that I never saw her in the company of po' whitefolks. For since they tend to think of the whiteness as an evenizer, I'm certain that I would have had to hear her spoken to commonly as Bertha, and my image of her would have been shattered like the unmendable Humpty-Dumpty.

One summer afternoon, sweet-milk fresh in my memory, she stopped at the Store to buy provisions. Another Negro woman of her health and age would have been expected to carry the paper sacks home in one hand, but

Momma said, "Sister Flowers, I'll send Bailey up to your house with these things."

She smiled that slow dragging smile, "Thank you, Mrs. Henderson, I'd prefer Marguerite, though." My name was beautiful when she said it. "I've been meaning to talk to her, anyway." They gave each other age-group looks.

Momma said, "Well, that's all right then. Sister go and change your dress. You going to Sister Flowers."

The chifforobe was a maze. What on earth did one put on to go to Mrs. Flowers' house? I knew I shouldn't put on a Sunday dress. It might be sacrilegious. Certainly not a house dress, since I was already wearing a fresh one. I chose a school dress, naturally. It was formal without suggesting that going to Mrs. Flowers' house was equivalent to attending church.

I trusted myself back into the Store.

"Now, don't you look nice." I had chosen the right thing, for once.

"Mrs. Henderson, you make most of the children's clothes, don't you?"

"Yes, ma'am. Sure do. Store-bought clothes ain't hardly worth the thread it take to stitch them."

"I'll say you do a lovely job, though, so neat. That dress looks professional."

Momma was enjoying the seldom-received compliments. Since everyone we knew (except Mrs. Flowers, of course) could sew competently, praise was rarely handed out for the commonly practiced craft.

"I try, with the help of the Lord, Sister Flowers, to finish the inside just like I does the outside. Come here, Sister."

I had buttoned up the collar and tied the belt, apron-like, in back. Momma told me to turn around. With one hand she pulled the strings, and the belt fell free at both sides of my waist. Then her large hands were at my neck, opening the button loops. I was terrified. What was happening?

"Take it off, Sister." She had her hands on the hem of the dress.

"I don't need to see the inside, Mrs. Henderson, I can tell. . . ." But the dress was over my head and my arms were stuck in the sleeves. Momma said, "That'll do. See here, Sister Flowers, I French-seams around the arm-holes." Through the cloth film, I saw the shadow approach. "That makes it last longer. Children these days would bust out of sheet-metal clothes. They so rough."

"That is a very good job, Mrs. Henderson. You should be proud. You can put your dress back on, Marguerite."

"No, ma'am. Pride is a sin. And 'cording to the Good Book, it goeth before a fall."

"That's right. So the Bible says. It's a good thing to keep in mind."

I wouldn't look at either of them. Momma hadn't thought that taking off my dress in front of Mrs. Flowers would kill me stone dead. If I had refused, she would have thought I was trying to be "womanish" . . . . Mrs. Flowers had known that I would be embarrassed and that was even worse. I picked up the groceries and went out to wait in the hot sunshine. It would be fitting if I got a sunstroke and died before they came outside. Just dropped dead on the slanting porch.

There was a little path beside the rocky road, and

Mrs. Flowers walked in front swinging her arms and picking her way over the stones.

She said, without turning her head, to me, "I hear you're doing very good school work, Marguerite, but that it's all written. The teachers report that they have trouble getting you to talk in class." We passed the triangular farm on our left, and the path widened to allow us to walk together. I hung back in the separate unasked and unanswerable questions.

"Come and walk along with me, Marguerite." I couldn't have refused even if I wanted to. She pronounced my name so nicely. Or more correctly, she spoke each word with such clarity that I was certain a foreigner who didn't understand English could have understood her.

"Now no one is going to make you talk—possibly no one can. But bear in mind, language is man's way of communicating with his fellow man and it is language alone which separates him from the lower animals." That was a totally new idea to me, and I would need time to think about it.

"Your grandmother says you read a lot. Every chance you get. That's good, but not good enough. Words mean more than what is set down on paper. It takes the human voice to infuse them with the shades of deeper meaning."

I memorized the part about the human voice infusing words. It seemed so valid and poetic.

She said she was going to give me some books and that I not only must read them. I must read them aloud. She suggested that I try to make a sentence sound in as many different ways as possible.

"I'll accept no excuse if you return a book to me that has been badly handled." My imagination boggled at the punishment I would deserve if in fact I did abuse a book of Mrs. Flowers'. Death would be too kind and brief.

The odors in the house surprised me. Somehow I had never connected Mrs. Flowers with food or eating or any other common experience of common people. There must have been an outhouse, but my mind never recorded it.

The sweet scent of vanilla had met us as she opened the door.

"I made tea cookies this morning. You see, I had planned to invite you for cookies and lemonade so we could have this little chat. The lemonade is in the icebox."

It followed that Mrs. Flowers would have ice on an ordinary day, when most families in our town bought ice late on Saturdays only a few times during the summer to be used in the wooden ice-cream freezers.

She took the bags from me and disappeared through the kitchen door. I looked around the room that I had never in my wildest fantasies imagined I would see. Browned photographs leered or threatened from the walls, and the white, freshly done curtains pushed against themselves and against the wind. I wanted to gobble up the room entire and take it to Bailey, who would help me analyze and enjoy it.

"Have a seat, Marguerite. Over there by the table." She carried a platter covered with a tea towel. Although she warned that she hadn't tried her hand at baking sweets for some time, I was certain that like everything else about her the cookies would be perfect.

They were flat round wafers, slightly browned on the edges and butter-yellow in the center. With the cold lemonade they were sufficient for childhood's lifelong diet. Remembering my manners, I took nice little ladylike bites

off the edges. She said she had made them expressly for
me and that she had a few in the kitchen that I could take
home to my brother. So I jammed one whole cake in my
mouth and the rough crumbs scratched the insides of my
jaws, and if I hadn't had to swallow, it would have been a
dream come true.

As I ate she began the first of what we later called "my
lessons in living." She said that I must always be intoler-
ant of ignorance but understanding of illiteracy. That
some people, unable to go to school, were more educated
and even more intelligent than college professors. She encouraged me to listen carefully to what country people
called mother wit. That in those homely sayings was
couched the collective wisdom of generations.

When I finished the cookies she brushed off the table
and brought a thick, small book from the bookcase. I had
read *A Tale of Two Cities* and found it up to my standards as
a romantic novel. She opened the first page and I heard
poetry for the first time in my life.

"It was the best of times and the worst of times. . . ."
Her voice slid in and curved down through and over the
words. She was nearly singing. I wanted to look at the
pages. Were they the same that I had read? Or were there
notes, music, lined on the pages, as in a hymn book? Her
sounds began cascading gently. I knew from listening to a
thousand preachers that she was nearing the end of her
reading, and I hadn't really heard, heard to understand, a
single word.

"How do you like that?"

It occurred to me that she expected a response. The
sweet vanilla flavor was still on my tongue and her reading was a wonder in my ears. I had to speak.

I said, "Yes, ma'am." It was the least I could do, but it was the most also.

"There's one more thing. Take this book of poems and memorize one for me. Next time you pay me a visit, I want you to recite."

I have tried often to search behind the sophistication of years for the enchantment I so easily found in those gifts. The essence escapes but the aura remains. To be allowed, no, invited, into the private lives of strangers, and to share their joys and fears, was a chance to exchange the Southern bitter wormwood for a cup of mead with Beowulf or a hot cup of tea and milk with Oliver Twist. When I said aloud, "It is a far, far better thing that I do, than I have ever done . . ." tears of love filled my eyes at my selflessness.

On that first day, I ran down the hill and into the road (fews cars ever came along it) and had the good sense to stop running before I reached the Store.

I was liked, and what a difference it made. I was respected, not as Mrs. Henderson's grandchild or Bailey's sister, for just being Marguerite Johnson.

Childhood's logic never asks to be proved (all conclusions are absolute). I didn't question why Mrs. Flowers had singled me out for attention, nor did it occur to me that Momma might have asked her to give me a little talking to. All I cared about was that she had made tea cookies for *me* and read to *me* from her favorite book. It was enough to prove that she liked me.

Momma and Bailey were waiting inside the Store. He said, "My, what did she give you?" He had seen the books, but I held the paper sack with his cookies in my arms shielded by the poems.

Momma said, "Sister, I know you acted like a little lady. That do my heart good to see settled people take to you all. I'm trying my best Lord knows, but these days. . . ." Her voice trailed off. "Go on in and change your dress."

LISTEN CHILDREN

listen children
keep this in the place
you have for keeping
always
keep it all ways

we have never hated black

listen
we have been ashamed
hopeless   tired   mad
but always
all ways
we loved us

we have always loved each other
children   all ways

pass it on

Lucille Clifton

FROM *WILMA*

Wilma Rudolph

Wilma Rudolph remembers being "the most sickly kid" in Clarksville, Tennessee. Though she spent most of her early years wearing a leg brace, when she was sixteen she won the bronze medal in track in the 1956 Olympics. At eighteen, Wilma became a mother, and it seemed as if her career in track was over. But in 1960, Wilma Rudolph became the first American woman to win three gold medals.

This part of Wilma's story takes place before her first Olympics, when she was still learning what being a winner really meant.

—D.S.S.

So it's 1956, and I'm a fifteen-year-old high school sopho-
more, and my life has never been better. I couldn't remember being happier. School was fun then. I remember
the television show "American Bandstand" was very big
with the kids, and once a week somebody would come
into the school with a bunch of records and we'd have our
own "American Bandstand" show after school. They
would give out records to kids who won dance contests
doing the latest dances, and I even won a couple myself.
All the girls were wearing long, tight skirts, the ones that
ended just below the knees, and bobby socks and padded
bras. They wore chains around their necks with their boy-
friends' rings on them, and if you were going steady with
an athlete, the girl wore the guy's letter sweaters or their
team jackets. Little Richard was big, and Chuck Berry was
big, but truthfully, Elvis Presley had no effect whatsoever.
Burt High School was all black, and we just didn't have
any kids in the school who identified with Elvis Presley.
The black kids sort of knew that he was just a white guy
singing black music, but no black kids had motorcycles or
leather jackets, probably because they didn't have the
money to buy them.

    We had all sorts of little social groups in the school,
but none that could be described as being like white greas-
ers. One group was the dressers, the kids who came from
fairly affluent homes and who showed it off by wearing
the best clothes all the time, even to the point where some

of the guys in this group came to school wearing suits and ties. The next group was the regulars, the kids who were looked upon as being regular kids, nothing special, just everyday happy kids. Athletes were another group and they usually stuck with other athletes. The funniest group was the "process" guys. They would go to barber shops and get their hair straightened, and everybody would talk about how the barbers used lye to straighten out their hair. Then they would slick back the straightened hair, and this slick look became known as the "Process Look." The guys thought it gave them a worldly image, the image of being real slick dudes who hung around in nightclubs and traveled with the fastest company. But most of them did just the opposite; they traveled with other process guys only.

My whole life at the time revolved around basketball and my family. Robert was my boyfriend; we went out on dates, and when there was nothing else to do, we'd all go hang out at the local teen-age club. Life seemed so uncomplicated, and happy, then.

As soon as the basketball season ended, I had my track stuff on, and I was running. There was a kid in school everybody called "Sundown"; the reason he was called that was because he was so black. His real name was Edward. Anyway, he and I used to skip out of classes almost every day, and we'd sneak off across the street to the municipal stadium, and we'd throw our books over the big wall that surrounded the stadium, then we'd climb the fence and run over to the track and do some running. If we heard any strange sounds, like somebody was coming, we'd run underneath the stands and hide.

Sometimes, when the college track team from Austin

Peay College was using the stadium, the place would be filled with these white guys practicing. "Sundown" and I would show up out of the clear blue sky, and they would look, and sort of blink and then go back about their business. The coach of the college team, this white guy, sort of knew that I was skipping out of classes to practice running; he would give me this little wink, like he knew what was going on but like he also had a little bit of admiration for me because I was so in love with running. Whenever he talked to his team, I would sort of hang around on the fringes and listen, hoping to pick up a pointer or two for free. I think he noticed that, too, and when he saw me sort of hanging around, it always seemed he would start talking a little louder than before.

That taste of winning I had gotten the year before never left me. I was more serious about track now, thinking deep down inside that maybe I had a future in the sport if I tried hard enough. So I thought nothing of cutting classes and going out to run. But one day I got a call to report to the principal's office. I went in, and he said, "Wilma, all of us here know just how important running track is to you. We all know it, and we are all hoping that you become a big success at it. But you can't keep cutting classes and going out to run." I was, well, mortified; the principal had found me out. He finally said that if I continued cutting classes, he would have to tell my father, and I knew what that meant. So I stopped. Even so, I was the first girl out there at practice and the last one to leave, I loved it so. We had some more of those playday-type meets early that season, and I kept on winning all the races I was in. I felt unbeatable.

Then came the big meet at Tuskegee, Alabama. It was

the big meet of the year. Girls from all over the South were invited down there to run, and the competition was the best for high school kids. It was a whole weekend type of thing, and they had dances and other things planned for the kids when they weren't out running. Coach Gray was going to drive us all down there to Tuskegee Institute, where the meet was held, and I remember we brought our very best dresses. We all piled into his car until there wasn't an inch of empty space in that car. Mrs. Allison, my old teacher, came with us; she was going to chaperon us at the big dance after the meet.

All the way down to Alabama, we talked and laughed and had a good time, and Coach Gray would tell us how tough the competition was going to be, especially the girls from Atlanta, Georgia, because they had a lot of black schools down there, and they had these track programs that ran the whole year because of the warm weather. When we got there, all of us were overwhelmed, because that was the first college campus any of us ever saw. We stayed in this big dorm, and I remember just before the first competition, I started getting this nervous feeling that would stay with me for the rest of my running career. Every time before a race, I would get it, this horrible feeling in the pit of my stomach, a combination of nerves and not eating.

When we got to the track, these girls from Georgia really looked like runners, but I paid them no mind because, well, I was a little cocky. I did think I could wipe them out because, after all, I had won every single race I had ever been in up to that point. So what happens? I got wiped out. It was the absolute worst experience of my life. I did not win a single race I ran in, nor did I qualify for anything. I was totally crushed. The girls from Georgia won everything. It was the first time I had ever tasted defeat in track, and it left me a total wreck. I was so despondent that I refused to go to any of the activities that were planned, including the big dance. I can't remember ever being so totally crushed by anything.

On the ride back, I sat in the car and didn't say a word to anybody, I just thought to myself about how much work was ahead of me and how I would like nothing better in the whole world than to come back to Tuskegee the next year and win everything. When I got home, my father knew immediately what had happened, and he didn't say anything. Every time I used to come home after a meet, I would rush into the house all excited and bubble over with, "I won . . . I won." This time I didn't say a word. I just walked in quietly, nodded to my father who was sitting there, and went into my room and unpacked.

After so many easy victories, using natural ability alone, I got a false sense of being unbeatable. But losing to those girls from Georgia, who knew every trick in the book, that was sobering. It brought me back down to earth, and it made me realize that I couldn't do it on natural ability alone, that there was more to track than just running fast. I also realized it was going to test me as a person—could I come back and win again after being so totally crushed by a defeat?

When I went back to school, I knew I couldn't continue to cut classes to practice or else I'd be in big trouble. So I would fake sickness, tell the teacher that I didn't feel well and could I please go home? They would let me go, and then I would go over to the track and run. When that stopped working, when they realized that I looked pretty good for being sick all the time, I simply asked them point-blank, "Look, could I cut this class today and go out and run?" Believe it or not, a lot of teachers said, "Okay, Wilma, go, but don't tell anybody."

I ran and ran and ran every day, and I acquired this sense of determination, this sense of spirit that I would never, never give up, no matter what else happened. That day at Tuskegee had a tremendous effect on me inside. That's all I ever thought about. Some days I just wanted to go out and die. I just moped around and felt sorry for myself. Other days I'd go out to the track with fire in my eyes, and imagine myself back at Tuskegee, beating them all. Losing as badly as I did had an impact on my personality. Winning all the time in track had given me confidence; I felt like a winner. But I didn't feel like a winner any more after Tuskegee. My confidence was shattered and I was thinking the only way I could put it all together was to get back the next year and wipe them all out.

But looking back on it all, I realized somewhere along the line that to think that way wasn't necessarily right, that it was kind of extreme. I learned a very big lesson for the rest of my life as well. The lesson was, winning is great, sure, but if you are really going to do something in life, the secret is learning how to lose. Nobody goes undefeated all the time. If you can pick up after a crushing defeat, and go on to win again, you are going to be a champion someday. But if losing destroys you, it's all over. You'll never be able to put it all back together again.

I did, almost right away. There were more playdays scheduled, and I won all the rest of the races I was in the rest of that season. But I never forgot Tuskegee. In fact, I was thinking that anybody who saw me lose so badly at the meet would write me off immediately. I was wrong. One day, right after the track season ended that year,

Coach Gray came over to me and he said, "Wilma, Ed Temple, the referee who is the women's track coach at Tennessee State, is going to be coming down to Clarksville to talk with your mother and father."

"What about?" I asked.

"Wilma," he said, "I think he wants you to spend the summer with him at the college, learning the techniques of running."

FROM *THE STORY OF STEVIE WONDER*

James Haskins

"Growing Up in a World of Darkness"

"See, about sound . . . ," Stevie Wonder says, "there's one thing you gotta remember about sound—sound happens all the time, *all* the time. If you put your hands right up to your ears, if you close your eyes and move your hands back and forth, you can hear the sound getting closer and farther away. . . . Sound bounces off everything, there's always something happening."

Stevie Wonder was born Steveland Morris on May 13, 1950, in Saginaw, Michigan. He was the third boy in a family that would eventually include five boys and one girl. All except Stevie were born without handicaps. He was born prematurely, and his early birth led to his total blindness.

"I guess that I first became aware that I was blind," Stevie recalls "—and I just vaguely remember this—when I'd be wallowing around in the grass back of the house, and I'd get myself and my clothes soiled. My mother would get on me about that. She explained that I couldn't move about so much, that I'd have to try and stay in one place.

"When I was young," he says, "my mother taught me never to feel sorry for myself, because handicaps are really things to be used, another way to benefit yourself and others in the long run." This was the best possible advice Stevie's mother could have given. He learned to regard his blindness in more than one way. It could be a hindrance, but it could also be a special gift. He was able to accept this idea, sometimes better than his mother could.

"I know it used to worry my mother," Stevie recalls, "and I know she prayed for me to have sight someday, and so finally I just told her that I was *happy* being blind, and I thought it was a gift from God, and I think she felt better after that."

Stevie was a lucky child in many ways. He was lucky to have two brothers close enough to him in age not to understand at first about his blindness and to expect him to do many of the things they did. He was also lucky to have a mother and a father, and occasionally an uncle, who understood how important sound was to him, and how important it was for him to learn to identify things he could not see by their sound. He recalls:

"I remember people dropping money on the table and saying, 'What's that, Steve?' That's a dime—buh-duh-duh-da; that's a quarter—buh-duh-duh-duh-da; that's a nickel. I could almost always get it right except a penny and a nickel confused me.

"I don't really feel my hearing is any better than yours," Stevie says now; "we all have the same abilities,

you know. The only difference is how much you use it."
Encouraged by his family, Stevie used his hearing more
and more as he grew older. He learned how to tell birds
apart by their call, and to tell trees apart by the sound their
leaves made as they rustled in the wind. He learned to tell
when people were tired or annoyed or pleased by listening to the tone of their voices. His world of sound grew
larger and larger, and the most frightening experience for
him was silence. He depended so on sound that silence,
for him, was like total darkness for deaf children. It is hard
for sighted and hearing people to understand this.
Perhaps the best way to understand is to imagine being
shut up in a dark, soundproof box. People need to feel
that they are part of the world around them. It is hard
enough to do so when one cannot see, or when one cannot hear; but it is doubly hard for a blind person in a silent
room or a deaf person in total darkness.

He also spent a lot of time beating on things, to make
sounds and to make music. Although his mother was a
gospel singer, the family was not especially musical. But
Stevie had shown musical interest and ability very young.
By the time he was two years old his favorite toys were
two spoons, with which he would beat rhythmically on
pans and tabletops and anything else his mother would let
him beat on. When she began to worry about her furni-
ture, she bought him cardboard drums from the dime
store. None of them lasted very long. "I'd beat 'em to
death," Stevie says with a chuckle. But there would always be a new drum, and there were other toy instruments as well.

"One day someone gave me a harmonica to put on

my key chain, a little four-hole harmonica," Stevie recalls. He managed to get a remarkable range of sounds from that toy instrument.

"Then one day my mother took me to a picnic and someone sat me behind my first set of drums. They put my foot on the pedal and I played. They give me a quarter. I liked the sound of quarters."

At a very early age, too, Stevie began to sing. All voices were very important to him, for they brought him closer to the world around him, a world he could not see. As he grew older, his own voice became particularly important to him, especially at night when the rest of the house was silent. He learned the endless possibilities of the human voice by experimenting with his own, and by mimicking others'.

Music itself, not necessarily made by him, became very important to him. He loved to listen to the radio; his earliest memory is of hearing Johnny Ace singing "Pledging My Love" on the radio. Shortly before he entered school he was given a small transistor radio for his very own. From then on, that radio was his constant companion. He even slept with it under his pillow at night. It played softly, providing sounds for him in an otherwise silent apartment. When he started school, he insisted on taking it to school with him.

Stevie was enrolled in special classes for the blind in the Detroit public school system. A special bus picked him up every morning and brought him back every afternoon. Stevie wished he could walk to school as his brothers did, and go to their neighborhood school. But he was learning to adjust to the fact that he must lead a different life, and in his special classes he was taught many things that would help him lead as normal a life as possible.

Sighted children attended the same school, and they often whispered about "the blind kids" as they passed by. Adults did the same thing. Somehow, normal people have the idea that blind people cannot hear them. It was hard to deal in an honest way with sighted people or even with his partially sighted classmates.

Being blind is to be exposed to constant frustrations. Dropping something, especially something small, means having to grope about with little chance of finding it. Some blind children won't even bother looking for an object they have dropped because they are embarrassed to be seen groping about for it.

Stevie had an additional problem in getting along with other children. Not only was he blind; he was also black. At first it might seem that the idea of skin color should not be very important to a child who has never seen color. But blackness is not just skin color; it is a culture, a way of looking at things. People divide themselves into "Us" and "Them" because of skin color, but that is not the only division. We also divide ourselves because of religion, education, economic class. If everyone in the entire world were blind, people would still divide themselves into "Us" and "Them"; it just would not be on the basis of appearance.

At home, Stevie heard his brothers and their friends talk about the white kids they knew. Before long, even though Stevie could not himself see color, he was very aware of skin color, and in addition to being self-conscious because of his blindness he was a little bit ashamed of being black.

"I remember when I was little," says Stevie, "I used

to listen to this black radio station in Detroit on my way to school. Like I was the only black kid on the bus, and I would always turn the radio down, because I felt ashamed to let them hear me listening to B.B. King. But I *loved* B.B. King. Yet I felt ashamed because—because I was *different* enough to want to hear him and because I had never heard him anywhere else."

[Stevie] was not about to stop listening to B.B. King; he simply played his radio softly in situations where he felt uncomfortable. That radio meant more to him than just about anything else in the world.

"I spent a lot of time listening to the radio," Stevie recalls, "and I was able to relate to the different instruments and know what they were. I began to know them by name. I used to listen to this program on station WCHB . . . called 'Sundown.' The disc jockey was named Larry Dixon and he always played a lot of old songs. There was one thing he played, it was his theme song . . . da da duh duh *dommm* da duh . . . da da da da *dommm* *dommm* da da duh. . . . Oh, it's really a bad tune, really a beautiful song—can't think of the name right now, but I could never forget that tune."

He would sing the words of the songs quietly to himself. He would hum the tunes. He would tap out the beats on his toy drums and try to play the melodies on his four-note harmonica. It frustrated him not to have real, grown-up instruments to play on, and it was hard for him to accept the fact that his mother just did not have enough money to buy real instruments for him. But luck soon proved to be with Stevie. Within the space of about a year and a half, he managed to acquire not one but *three* real instruments.

Every year the Detroit Lions Club gave a Christmas

party for blind children, and at Christmastime during his first-grade year at school Stevie went to one. Each child received a gift, and someone must have told the Detroit Lions Club about Stevie's interest in music, for his gift—he could hardly believe it—was a set of real drums! Stevie sat down and began to pound on them right then and there.

[Later a neighborhood] barber gave Stevie a harmonica—a real one. He practiced and practiced until he had mastered that.

Then, when he was seven, Stevie became the proud owner of a real piano. A neighbor was moving out of the housing project, and she really did not want to take her piano. Knowing how much Stevie loved music, she decided to give it to him. Stevie remembers, "I kept asking, 'When they gonna bring the piano over, Mamma?' I never realized how important that was going to be to me." When the piano finally arrived, it was like all the birthdays Stevie could remember all rolled into one. He ran his hands along the smooth wooden top, down the sides and around the back, down the slim legs, around to the cold metal of the pedals, and back up to the keys, some flat, some raised. He asked his mother to open the top of the piano, so he could feel the strings inside. He asked her what color they were. They were kind of gold, and the small wooden blocks between them were light brown. What color was the piano? A dark brown. From that moment on, dark brown, although he had not ever seen it and would never see it, meant something nice to Stevie. And since, he had been told, his skin was a sort of dark brown, too, he began to feel much better about his skin color.

By the time he was nine or ten Stevie was a very popular member of the neighborhood. He was certainly the most gifted musically, and he spent many Saturdays and after-school hours on the front porches of neighbors' houses on Horton Street. By this time Stevie had a set of bongo drums, which he had mastered as he had every other instrument to which he had been exposed. Often he would play his bongos; sometimes it would be the harmonica. Everyone would join in the singing, but Stevie's clear, strong voice always took the lead. Without exception the music was rhythm and blues, the kind the people listened to on WCHB.

One of his favorite singing partners was a boy about his age named John Glover. John Glover had a grown-up cousin named Ronnie White, who lived in another part of the city. Ronnie White was a member of the singing group the Miracles, which had enjoyed great success recording with a company named Hitsville USA. Of course, John Glover was very proud to have a cousin like Ronnie White, and he often boasted about him. John Glover was also proud to have a friend like Stevie. "You oughta hear my friend Stevie," he kept telling his cousin. But naturally White was busy, and he didn't really believe this kid Stevie was anything special. Then, one day in 1960, he happened to drop by to visit his relatives on Horton Street, and Stevie just happened to be having one of his front-porch sessions at the time. White did not have to listen very long to realize that his little cousin was right. This kid was something!

White arranged with the president of Hitsville USA, Berry Gordy, to take Stevie to the company's recording studio and to give him an audition, and one exciting afternoon Stevie was taken to the place that would be like a second home to him for the next ten years.

Stevie will never forget that afternoon. White took

him around the studio, helping him to the different instruments and sound equipment, letting him touch them. It
seemed to Stevie that every wonderful instrument in the
world was right there in that sound studio, and he never
wanted to leave it. Then he was introduced to Berry
Gordy. Gordy listened to him sing, and play the harmonica and drums, and hired him on the spot, which says a lot
for Gordy. Few, if any, other record-company owners
would have taken such a chance back in 1960. But then,
few, if any, other record companies had or would have the
history of Gordy's. No other black-owned label would pre-
vail as his would, and perhaps this was because once they
were established, those other labels were too busy holding
on to their position to take any risk or to try anything new.

Anyway, signing an artist brought in by a performer
already with the company has become a common, and
famous, practice of Gordy's. The Supremes were discovered by the Temptations. Diana Ross discovered the
Jackson Five.

Of course, Stevie's mother actually signed Stevie's
contract with Hitsville, for he was underage. There was
little talk of money or other conditions. Stevie's family was
so excited, so grateful for this opportunity for him, that
they would have agreed to anything!

DECEMBER

"The end of a thing
is never the end,
something is always
being born like
a year or a baby."

"I don't understand,"
Everett Anderson says.
"I don't understand where
the whole thing's at."

"It's just about Love,"
his Mama smiles.
"It's all about Love and
you know about that."

Lucille Clifton

THE CONTRIBUTORS

VERNA AARDEMA was born in Michigan and attended elementary school and college there. She now lives in Muskegon, Michigan, where she teaches second grade and is the City Staff Correspondent for the *Muskegon Chronicle*. She is the author of a number of books of African folktales including *Tales for the Third Ear*, *Behind the Back of the Mountain*, *Why Mosquitoes Buzz in People's Ears*, and *Who's in Rabbit's House?* (p. 42)

MAYA ANGELOU grew up in the little town of Stamps, Arkansas. As a young woman she studied dance in San Francisco and toured Europe and Africa for the State Department in *Porgy and Bess*. She is the author of *I Know Why the Caged Bird Sings*, *Gather Together in My Name*, *Singin' and Swingin' and Gettin' Merry Like Christmas*, and several books of poetry. In addition to writing and dancing, she has also produced and directed television programs. (p. 83)

KATHLEEN ARNOTT has collected folktales from every part of the world. She has compiled four books of African folklore: *African Myths and Legends*; *Dragons, Ogres, and Scary Things*; *Spiders, Crabs, and Creepy Crawlers*; and *Tales of Temba*. (p. 31)

GWENDOLYN BROOKS was born in Topeka, Kansas, in 1917. She has published a novel and nine volumes of poetry, including *Bronzeville Boys and Girls*. Her book of poems about black life in Chicago, *Annie Allen*, received the 1950 Pulitzer Prize for

113

Poetry. She is Distinguished Professor of Arts at the City College of New York as well as Poet Laureate of Illinois. She now lives in Chicago where she was raised. (p. 4)

ALICE CHILDRESS was born in Charleston, South Carolina, and raised in Harlem, New York. She has written plays, novels, and short stories. She is also an actress and a director. Among her many published works are two novels for young adults, *A Hero Ain't Nothin' but a Sandwich* (an ALA Notable Book) and *Rainbow Jordan*; and the play, *When the Rattlesnake Sounds*. (p. 54)

LUCILLE CLIFTON was born in Depew, New York, in 1936. She has written many storybooks and collections of poems for children including *Some of the Days of Everett Anderson, Everett Anderson's Year, The Black B C's*, and *The Boy Who Didn't Believe in Spring*. An award-winning poet, she frequently reads her poetry for audiences at colleges and universities. She lives in Baltimore with her husband and six children. (pp. 93 and 111)

NIKKI GIOVANNI was born in Knoxville, Tennessee, in 1943. She grew up in Cincinnati, Ohio, and attended Fisk University. She has written short stories, essays, and many books of poems including *Black Feeling, Black Talk/Black Judgement; Spin a Soft Black Song; My House;* and *ego-tripping and other poems for young people*. She has made recordings of her work and frequently gives poetry readings. She is the mother of a son, Tommy. (p. 82)

ELOISE GREENFIELD has lived in Washington, D.C., almost all her life. As a youngster she studied piano, sang with three friends in a group called the Langston Harmonettes, and won a citywide typing contest when she was fourteen. She went on to win many more prizes—for her writing. She has written more than a dozen books for young readers including *Paul Robeson, Rosa Parks, Africa Dream* (winner of the 1978 Coretta Scott King Award), *Honey, I Love and Other Poems* (a 1978 ALA Notable Book), and *Childtimes*. She has two children: a daughter, Monica, and a son, Steve. (pp. 3 and 70)

VIRGINIA HAMILTON was born in Yellow Springs, Ohio. Her grandfather Perry was a slave who escaped his bondage; she grew up in what had been one of the strongest stations of the Underground Railroad. She has written many books for young readers including four ALA Notable Books, *Zeely, The House of Dies Drear, The Planet of Junior Brown*, and *Time-Ago Tales of Jahdu; M.C. Higgins, the Great* (winner of the Newbery, National Book, and Boston Globe–Horn Book Awards), and the Justice Trilogy. She still lives in Yellow Springs with her husband and two children. (p. 5)

JAMES HASKINS has written many books for adults and young people. He has taught elementary school and junior high, and currently serves as Associate Professor of English at the University of Florida at Gainesville. Some of his books include *Diary of a Harlem Schoolteacher, Mysticism and Magic in the Black World, The Long Struggle, Werewolves*, and *The Story of Stevie Wonder* (winner of the Coretta Scott King Award). He now commutes weekly between Florida and his New York City apartment. (p. 102)

LANGSTON HUGHES devoted his life to writing and lecturing, and became one of the most important and versatile writers of the Harlem literary renaissance. Born in Joplin, Missouri, in 1902. he began writing poetry when he was in high school. His first book of poems, *The Weary Blues*, was published when he was twenty-four years old. Langston Hughes received international recognition and many awards including a Guggenheim Fellowship, a grant from the American Academy of Arts and Letters, and a decoration by Emperor Haile Selassie of Ethiopia. *The Dream Keeper* is a collection of his poems for children. Langston Hughes died in 1967. (pp. 30 and 52)

KRISTIN HUNTER was born in Philadelphia and still lives there. She was educated at the University of Pennsylvania. Her short stories and novels have won many awards. They include *Guests in the Promised Land* (a National Book Award nominee), *Boss Cat, The Soul Brothers and Sister Lou,* and *Lou in the Limelight.* (p. 18)

MARTIN LUTHER KING, JR. was a clergyman, author, civil rights leader and champion of nonviolence. Born and reared in Atlanta, Georgia, he married CORETTA SCOTT in 1953, and they had four children. Perhaps the most famous of his many awards for leadership was the Nobel Peace Prize which he received in 1964. He died from an assassin's bullet in 1968. (p. 75)

DON L. LEE was born in 1942 in Little Rock, Arkansas, and raised in Chicago. He has served as a staff member of The Museum of African-American History in Chicago, and has taught Afro-American literature in colleges and universities. He has written many books of poetry including *Think Black!, Black Pride,* and *We Walk the Way of the New World.* (p. 29)

DUDLEY RANDALL was born in Washington, D.C., in 1914. He received a master's degree in library science from the University of Michigan and has been a librarian, poet, and publisher of black American literature. His poetry collections include *Cities Burning, Love You,* and *More to Remember.* (p. 48)

WILMA RUDOLPH was born in 1940 in Clarksville, Tennessee, the nineteenth of twenty-one children. An outstanding college athlete, both in basketball and track, she became an Olympic champion runner. She and her husband have four children and reside in Clarksville. (p. 94)

SONIA SANCHEZ was born in Birmingham, Alabama, in 1935. She was educated at New York University and Hunter College. She has since lectured at colleges throughout the country, appeared on television programs featuring black poets, and authored many volumes of poetry. Her works include *Homecoming, We a Baddddd People, It's a New Day: Poems for Young Brothas and Sistuhs, Three Hundred and Sixty Degrees of Blackness Comin at You,* and *A Blues Book for Blue Black Magical Women.* She is one of the most influential contemporary black poets. (p. 17)

MARGARET WALKER was born the daughter of a minister in Birmingham, Alabama, in 1915. Her books of poetry include *For My People* (a Yale University Younger Poets volume), and *Prophets for a New Day.* Her novel, *Jubilee,* received the Houghton-Mifflin Literary Fellowship. She has been on the faculty of Jackson State College for many years. (p. 81)

HARRIET WHEATLEY'S poem, "My Pa Was Never Slave," appeared in *Black World* magazine in September 1973. (p. 53)

INDEX OF TITLES
by Genre

Poetry

ABOUT THE EDITOR

DOROTHY S. STRICKLAND received her Master of Arts degree in educational psychology and her Ph.D. in early childhood and elementary education at New York University. She has written numerous articles for educational journals, was the editor of the book *The Role of Literature in Reading Instruction*, and co-author of the Allyn & Bacon *Pathfinders* series. She has held elected offices in the National Council of Teachers of English and the International Reading Association. She was president of the I.R.A. during the 1978–79 term. Dr. Strickland is currently professor of education at Teachers College, Columbia University.

ABOUT THE ILLUSTRATORS

LEO AND DIANE DILLON are among the most highly re-spected illustrators in America today. The books they have illustrated include *The Hundred Penny Box*, which received the Newbery Medal; *Why Mosquitos Buzz in People's Ears: A West African Tale*, which received the Caldecott Medal for Children's Book Illustration in 1975; and *Ashanti to Zulu: African Traditions*, which received the Caldecott Medal, the *New York Times* Best Illustrated Children's Book Award and the Hamilton King Award in 1977. Their work has appeared in many magazines, including the *Ladies' Home Journal*, and the *Saturday Evening Post*. They have won the Hugo Award for Science Fiction Illustration. They are the subjects of *The Art of Leo and Diane Dillon*, a book which demonstrates the full range of their artistic style. The Dil-lons have one son, Leo, who helped in the preparation of the text illustrations for *Listen Children*.

Bantam Skylark Paperbacks
The Kid-Pleasers

Especially designed for easy reading with large type, wide margins and captivating illustrations, Skylarks are "kid-pleasing" paperbacks featuring the authors, subjects and characters children love.

15126	INCREDIBLE JOURNEY Sheila Burnford	$1.95
15097	CHARLIE AND THE CHOCOLATE FACTORY Roald Dahl	$2.25
15031	CHARLIE AND THE GREAT GLASS ELEVATOR Roald Dahl	$1.95
15113	JAMES AND THE GIANT PEACH Roald Dahl	$2.50
15138	ENCYCLOPEDIA BROWN BOY DETECTIVE Donald Sobol	$1.75
15140	ENCYCLOPEDIA BROWN CASE OF THE SECRET PITCH Donald Sobol	$1.75
15060	ABEL'S ISLAND William Steig	$1.95
15106	BIG RED Jim Kjelgaard	$2.25
15067	DRAGON, DRAGON AND OTHER TALES John Gardner	$1.75
15008	IRISH RED: SON OF BIG RED Jim Kjelgaard	$1.95
15086	JACOB TWO-TWO MEETS THE HOODED FANG Mordecai Richler	$1.95
15050	THE EYES OF THE AMARYLLIS Natalie Babbitt	$1.75
15065	TUCK EVERLASTING Natalie Babbitt	$1.95